READER REVIEWS

"The moment-to-moment practice of returning to a place of respect for self and respect for others is no longer an option. With burnout, stress, and mental health challenges on the continued rise, leading requires us to learn how to return to kindness and calm inside our minds so we can be effective in relationship to others. This inspiring and practical book shows us how."

—Susan MacKenty Brady,
Best-Selling Author & CEO,
The Simmons University Institute for Inclusive Leadership

"Straightforward, accessible, and honest, Christine shares her very personal journey into mindfulness and the transformative power of this ancient practice.

As a leadership coach she has worked with many leaders in a variety of industries and in this book has given them an opportunity to share their stories in their own voice and the profound impact the practice has had on them.

We learn how our mental habits shape our day-to-day experience and how there are different mindfulness practices we can tap into to address a particular need—whether that is to fully listen to another or simply bring ease to the body and mind during a stressful period. And each method includes clear and actionable steps. I simply loved this book—highly recommended!"

—Tara Healey, MEd.
Program Director Mind the Moment, Point32Health

"Christine's book is an exploration of mindfulness and the cultivation of a compassionate, balanced life. It offers a road map for anyone looking to transform their mental landscape from one filled with negativity to one characterized by acceptance, love, and understanding.

Christine's writing is not just theoretical; it is a practical guide filled with actionable techniques. From mastering the mind and practicing loving-kindness daily to silencing the inner critic and improving emotional intelligence, the book provides a comprehensive tool kit for personal transformation. The author encourages readers to focus on wholesome thoughts and let go of what they cannot control, reminding us of the impermanence and unpredictability of life.

For corporate professionals navigating high-stress environments, this book is a must-read. It equips you with the tools to enhance emotional intelligence, manage stress, and foster a positive workplace culture. By integrating these mindfulness practices, you can improve your leadership skills, increase resilience, and create a more harmonious work-life balance. Invest in your well-being and professional growth by picking up a copy today and start your journey towards a more mindful, effective, and fulfilling career."

—Brandi Dean,
Founder of The Dean Center for Tick Borne Illness, LLC

"Meditation is part of a broader way of life for me and many people who practice some form of Buddhism, so I'm always skeptical initially when I see it taken out of its broader context. Too often it gets packaged up for commercial consumption with guarantees of producing (superficially) shinier selves and organizations, rather than helping us see and channel the light that shines through each of us and all things. Christine O'Shaughnessy's book is refreshingly different. She embraces the paradox that we're more likely to experience meditation's greatest gifts if we settle into practice for the long haul 'without any expectation of the outcome.' And, yes, along the way it might just help us learn to deeply appreciate our lives and to be more capable and compassionate leaders."

—Jeff Kōgen Seul, Rōshi, *Full Moon Zen*

"Christine has delivered a powerful resource for all leaders who need to strengthen their muscles of resilience and align their intentions with their impact. A must-read rich with relevant insights and practical application for today's leaders."

—Kerry Seitz,
Vice President Women's Leadership,
Simmons University Institute for Inclusive Leadership

"If you are beginning a journey of self-awareness and authentic leadership, start here. Through a mix of personal experiences and practical advice, Christine talks humbly and fluidly of choice, control, surrender, freedom, health, and the wonderful strengths we all have inside.

Christine understands that modern leadership problems require age-old solutions. This book will help you open the door to find these solutions for yourself, along a personalized journey that can begin in a few small, simple steps. And if you are already a seasoned practitioner of mindfulness, you will find here new facets of inspiration and understanding about your own practice.

Mindful Presence in Leadership deserves its place among the best modern leadership advice out there, and should be required reading for those who want to walk more mindfully and lead more effectively."

—Jill Marie Lynch,
Talent Director, The Bicester Collection

"A succinct and extremely worthwhile read! The content contained within serves as reminders of the tools Christine has shared to restore balance and clarity in my life. Taming the inner critic is a particular challenge for me; namely the imposter syndrome…am I really that good? It's easy to fall in that mindset within the male-dominated investment advisory field where I have worked the last 40 years. With Christine's guidance of acknowledging and accepting its existence, I work hard not to let it define me. Taking the time to take literal deep breaths to calm my mind has helped me reinforce my authentic self and know I earned a seat at the table. Additionally, and more importantly, I have gained perspective with the things in life that are truly important: love, health, and happiness."

—Barbara F Letvinchuk, CFP® | Senior Vice President, Financial Advisor, RBC Wealth Management, A Division of RBC Capital Markets, LLC

"Christine O'Shaughnessy's new book, *Mindful Presence in Leadership: Releasing Burnout, Chaos, and Stress,* is a quick, easy, practical guide for all leaders. Christine draws on her background in the business world and her extensive experience as a mindfulness coach to deliver a warm and personal invitation to begin a mindfulness practice. Her straightforward and pragmatic approach is welcoming in a space that is, at times, cluttered with esoteric thinking and theory. Her data-driven approach and real-life case studies offer up mindfulness as a valuable and effective tool for those seeking professional and personal growth. Christine's take on the realities of the business world are spot on. We in the business world would be better leaders if we did as Christine suggests and practice a bit of loving-kindness and compassion. The book is a gem."

—Lynn Bowman, Senior Vice President, Service and Experience, Point32Health

"Mindful Presence in Leadership is a fantastic book and a must read for anyone interested in learning about meditation. Christine O'Shaughnessy has done an amazing job walking the reader through how and why to create a meditation practice for themselves. She provides captivating testimonials from leaders whose lives have been transformed through meditation and she teaches the reader how different meditation techniques can help with different challenges all while providing practical action steps and guidance. Her gentle presentation of her extensive experience in the field leaves the reader feeling more calm and relaxed just by reading it. She is a true leader in her field and this book is a treasure."

—Patty S Fallone
Parent Coach and author of the international best seller,
"How To Survive Your Child's Addiction - A Guide To Recovering Peace And Rediscovering Joy".

"Christine has written a masterful guide to meditation. A practical, easy step-by-step process to activate one's internal guidance system, strengthening the logical mind and calming the emotions. Whether in business or one's personal life, a sense of calm and safety is always a welcomed state. I believe that this book is a must-read for anyone looking to become their best self."

—Jill Halligan,
Neurological Integration System Master Practitioner
and CEO Halligan Wellness, LLC

"Mindfulness training with Christine was a valuable tool in communicating and working well with fellow employees. In HR, an employee approaches you with a question that is very important to them. The answer may not be what they hope. Mindfulness provided a way to improve the interaction. It provided pause to remind you to listen with empathy and to provide a space for the employee to be heard. This book will be a valuable tool for HR leaders to learn how to cultivate empathy and improve communications with employees."

—Kathy Holmquest, HR

"Mindfulness influences everything that comes within its reach, and leadership is only one of countless part of work life where its influence can be felt. A mindful leader is not only more effective (as O'Shaughnessy deftly argues), but becomes a beacon of wise attention, presence and clear communication in a way that is of benefit to everyone. Mindfulness deeply informs leadership, but is extends limitlessly into all facets of life.

There are countless books on management that identify the qualities of an effective leader. In most, concepts and advice fall to the ground before reaching the trainee's ear, much less resulting in genuine transformation. This volume provides practical advice on *how* to get there, offered with the authority of one who knows from personal experience and practice.

If all leaders practiced in the manner described by the author, the workplace might become a vehicle for personal and collective growth, rather than its semblance to a battleground."

—Paul R. Fulton
Institute for Meditation & Psychotherapy

"Any person reading this will be able to benefit from the tools and skills outlined in these pages. The hardest part is starting and staying committed to cultivating a meditation practice. I truly believe the world would be a better place if we all gave it a try. These pages provide a terrific overview and motivation to just begin. There are terrific lessons in these pages that can help all of us to be more connected, empathetic leaders within our jobs and the many roles we play in life."

—Elizabeth Bride

"The author begins by asking: who wouldn't want a healthy, sustainable mind? This book allows the reader to begin that journey. It is a journey toward freedom and power. It is the freedom to choose how *you* wish to interact with the world around you, and the power for *you* to choose to become the best version of yourself. This book also sends you down the path of a miracle. If you follow what the book teaches, you will discover that, the more you change, the more your world changes around you, beginning a virtuous cycle that never comes to an end."

—Josh Krumholz, Lawyer

MINDFUL PRESENCE

in

LEADERSHIP

Releasing
Burnout, Chaos, and Stress

CHRISTINE
O'SHAUGHNESSY

Hasmark
PUBLISHING
INTERNATIONAL

Editor: Brad Green (brad@hasmarkpublishing.com)
Cover Design: Anne Karklins (anne@hasmarkpublishing.com)
Art work: Rabea Stenger, RK Group, (rabea.k.stenger@web.de)
Interior Layout: Amit Dey (amit@hasmarkpublishing.com)

ISBN 13: 978-1-77482-294-4
ISBN 10: 1-77482-294-6

Hasmark
INTERNATIONAL

DEDICATION

This book is dedicated to my children Grace and Liam, my greatest teachers. May you always lead from your heart.

and

To all beings everywhere. May we all be free, peaceful, and at ease in our hearts and minds. May the teachings in this book spread light without ending and dissolve confusion and suffering.

TABLE OF CONTENTS

"A crowded mind leaves no space for a peaceful heart."

~ Christine Evangelou

FOREWORD

In a world that often feels chaotic and demanding, the pursuit of mindfulness and success can seem daunting. However, Christine's book is a beacon of hope and a practical guide for anyone seeking to cultivate a more peaceful, collaborative, and successful life. This is more than just a book; it is an essential resource that provides actionable steps and valuable education to elevate your awareness and transform your approach to life.

What I appreciated most about Christine's writing is the clarity with which she outlines the action steps. They are not only easy to implement but also deeply impactful. Throughout the book, Christine shares relatable examples from her own life and the lives of her clients, which vividly illustrate the effectiveness of these practices. As a mindset mentor, Buddhist practitioner, and seasoned meditation and yoga teacher, I have personally adopted many of these techniques with remarkable success.

Christine is truly a beacon of authentic, heart-centered service. Her wisdom and insights shine through every page, making this book a significant contribution to the field of mindfulness and personal development. I wholeheartedly recommend it to everyone looking to enhance their journey toward success and fulfillment.

Best regards,
Tara Pilling
Diamond Mind Consulting
Mindset Consultant, Speaker, Author, Ayurveda Coach,
Meditation Teacher

INTRODUCTION

"Our goal in this practice is not to extinguish all thoughts, but to change our relationship to the thinking mind, maybe even befriend it… Thoughts are not the enemy, they're a naturally arising phenomenon in the mind. We're just trying to learn about them, how they work, and how this world gets created for us through them."

~ Anushka Fernandopulle

Leadership and mindfulness may seem mutually exclusive. However, to be an effective leader, one must maintain a clear mind. In my 25 years of working in mindfulness and from seeing shifts resulting from my practice, I have observed a notable transformation in leaders who embrace meditation and its benefits. To lead others, you must first know yourself and understand who you are. Only by taking control of your own life can you lead others effectively. If you can't control yourself, how will you lead others? Cultivate your inner leadership by examining your mind and understanding how it shapes your behavior.

This book is designed for anyone seeking to understand how their mind operates and to apply the tools I provide. It is particularly aimed at those in leadership roles, encouraging them to lead more from the heart and less from the ego. It's about learning to calm the mind and observe your thoughts and responses. Mindfulness allows us to see thoughts as they arise and dissipate without engaging with them. Reframing our thoughts and avoiding harmful or unskillful speech and actions are crucial for leaders. The mind can either rest in compassion and understanding or dwell in chaos, stress, and burnout. This book will guide you to choose compassion and understanding as your foundation. It equips you to stand strong amid life's challenges with unshakable balance, wise responsiveness, and poise.

You will learn various techniques to support you in both leadership and in life. You will explore what it means to train the mind to cultivate ease and well-being, positioning yourself to lead with self-confidence, courage, and kindness. Through mindfulness, you will build trust among those who follow you, whether they are coworkers, friends, parents, or children.

Leaders distinguish themselves by taking action where others hesitate, starting with self-awareness and self-control. Developing inner leadership is essential, encompassing a deep understanding of one's mind, behavior, and attitude. This internal strength fosters courage, self-confidence, and a positive outlook. Effective leaders inspire and make others feel valued.

Over the years, many people have asked me how I've persevered despite all I have been through. Life has not always been easy. I have endured years of hardship, despair, and intense challenges—both physically and emotionally—due to family conditions and circumstances that left me exhausted and depleted. My answer to this question is always the same: I persevered through my meditation practice.

I used to work at an investment firm as a vice president and senior credit analyst. During my time there, I became ill, bedridden with stomach pain, unable to think or focus due to a clouded mind, chronic fatigue, exhaustion, and intense anger at my situation. I was out of work for six months. Doctors were baffled, and after a year of tests and scans, they suspected I might have cancer. Although I had a physical autoimmune condition and heavy metal toxicity, I later realized that most of my suffering stemmed from my own mental anguish. The state of our mind influences our body and shapes its physical condition over time.

I am eternally grateful to my director at that time who recommended I take Jon Kabat-Zinn's eight-week mindfulness-based stress reduction (MBSR) class. Initially, I was reluctant. It was my first introduction to meditation, yoga, and mindfulness. It was my first introduction to training my mind and understanding that the root of my suffering was optional. It was optional because the root was *my thinking* and my response to the physical and mental conditions that were arising. It was optional because I could change my thoughts. My director believed that part of my illness was work stress-related and that if I learned to manage or let go of that stress, I would be more productive and happier. Striving to climb the corporate ladder at the investment firm while completing my MBA at night led to countless all-night work sessions, living on caffeine, sugar, and minimal sleep. My immune system was depleted and needed recovery.

I remember arriving at my first MBSR class and listening to others share their stories and reasons for being there. When it was my turn to speak, I simply said, "I'm just stressed." I didn't believe I fit in there. Others were dealing with deeper issues like terminal illness, suicidal thoughts, addiction, and many other serious conditions. I was "just" stressed. I didn't see the connection between stress and its effects on my physical body and mind.

Over a period of eight weeks, I learned how to sit with the thoughts in my mind and the discomfort in my body, including overwhelming fatigue, pain, and internal suffering. We immersed ourselves in mindfulness teachings and practices that date back over 2,500 years. The last session of the eight weeks was an all-day silent retreat. I remember thinking, "I can't do that. It'll be torture!" My mind came up with all the reasons why it was foolish, harmful, and ridiculous to do this. What I was experiencing was fear, though at the time I didn't realize it. My mind concocted stories about why it wasn't good for me, and I believed them. It ended up being my favorite part of the MBSR experience. I now attend two-week silent retreats at least once or twice a year, and I cherish them.

After the first all-day silent retreat, I said to a friend, "Why doesn't everybody do this? And why aren't more corporations offering these types of trainings?"

What I had learned through the experience was that my body was an instrument of my mind. My body had become sick partly due to mental overwhelm, which included not having all the answers, striving, perfectionism, and self-preservation, all mindsets deeply ingrained from living in a challenging mental environment in my youth (requiring me to live in survival mode). I was inspired by the realization that training to create stability of mind would be of immense value to corporations. I had experienced firsthand that my mind was either orderly or confused, and it became clear that improving mental faculties is the most important education and one that is not taught in school. Each employee is only as valuable as the health of their mind. We're not able to focus, concentrate, lead, problem-solve, strategize, or be creative when we have a stressed, overwhelmed, and chaotic mind. I committed to finding a way to bring these teachings into corporations.

The skills cultivated through training the mind are invaluable and directly correlate with successful leadership. If we don't understand how our mind works and why we respond as we do, we live from habit, acting and responding in the same ways and getting the same results. Corporations will thrive with emotionally intelligent leaders who can manage stress, create, innovate, adapt to change, and think globally while being resilient and empathetic. Leaders must know how to manage their egos and lead from the heart. Corporations that employ and promote mindfulness training create healthier, more productive, harmonious work environments.

Over the past 25 years, I've led mindfulness and attention training programs for individual leaders and top professionals from a wide range of organizations, including Fortune 500 companies, non-profits, and universities, to help people thrive and develop self-awareness and leadership presence. Too many people fail to recognize the relationship between stress and the health of the physical and mental body. Scientific research has proven the benefits of reducing stress through mindfulness-based practices and training the mind to be at ease. There is an abundance of quantitative, evidence-based data demonstrating the advantages of adopting a mental training practice. When I began this endeavor in 1999, none of this was widely accepted, understood, or adopted. Fast forward 25 years, and the practice of mindfulness has become mainstream. Organizations offering mindfulness and meditation training include the World Economic Forum, Google, General Mills, the NBA, Target, SAP, and the United States Congress, to name a few.

In those years, I've committed to training my mind to rest in the teachings and to find equanimity. I will always be a student of this work, a practice that requires one to remain in a beginner's mindset. One doesn't "graduate" from this training; it is lifelong. I practice by rooting my mind in what is wholesome and moving away from what is unwholesome daily. What I mean by this is: do I want a mind full of acceptance, compassion, love, understanding, joy, empathy, and patience? Or do I want a mind full of aversion, resentment, bitterness, ill will, fear, and despair? We all have a choice of what type of mind we would like to cultivate. We can choose to train our mind to return to a place of wisdom and stillness, or we can allow it to fixate on obsession, perfectionism, anxiety, worry, and spinning. It isn't easy. It takes dedication, commitment, and effort to train the mind to rest in equanimity regardless of conditions. This is continuous work.

One of my clients, Jordan, a Managing Director at a Wall Street firm, shared his perspective:

> Over the past four years, I have led a busy life—raising three kids as a present father and husband, taking on more responsibility at a high-pressure job as a managing director, and recommitting to a physical and mental health regimen—all while learning to live life as a sober person. I have experienced the great joy that comes after the fog of substance use is lifted, but also the anguish of dealing with emotions that are now so acutely felt. Physical abstinence has done wonders, but it is only through mindfulness and meditation that I have learned to live life on life's terms and to trust in myself again. Sobriety alone does not make a strong leader, but I have been unrecognizable to myself in certain situations because of the serenity and perspective I gain from meditation. I used to cower and sweat before a year-end review. Now I am able to laugh and have been recognized as a stress absorber. At first, sobriety made meditation possible, but I am so grateful today that meditation is what keeps my sobriety possible.

Circumstances in life, cultural upbringings, and trauma all shape the nature of our minds. When we train the mind to rest in the heart, we see more clearly. By training the mind to be still, even for moments each day, we gain clarity. There is much to learn by sitting still and being silent. We learn to rest in the equilibrium of our hearts and move away from narrow-minded thinking, planning, controlling, and worrying. I learned all of this through my own hardships. We all come to these teachings in our own way, in our own time. It can't be forced.

This book is a compilation of the many teachings handed down to me from my teachers, mentors, and coaches. Its roots come from ancient traditions and wisdom shared over 2,500 years ago in the Buddhist tradition. I have chosen to share it now from my perspective, and in the way it has helped me to grow and evolve as a leader and as a human being. This work has allowed me to find peace in my life during difficult moments. It has helped me become a proactive leader rather than a reactive one. It is a grounding force that cannot be duplicated through any other practice.

This book is intended for leaders in the workplace, but the principles can certainly be applied at home, with family and friends, and in volunteer situations. By working with your mind, you enable yourself to live your best life. This work can be intimidating as it forces you to take an honest look at your true nature. I believe there is no other way to heal than by working through the constructs of your mind. My hope for you is that this book will ignite a spark in you to be brave and courageous in that exploration.

TRAINING THE MIND

Tricia's Story

Since the start of my meditation practice, I have noticed that I am more patient and less triggered by the actions of others in both my personal and professional life as an HR Partner. My daily practice involves taking the first five minutes of my morning commute to just sit in my seat on the train, breathe, and quiet my mind. I repeat this process as we approach the city. This practice has enabled me to enter the workday in a more positive manner, and I find myself being more productive and inclusive throughout the day. These traits are critical in a leadership role. Employees will mirror the actions of leaders, and keeping myself focused helps others follow suit. I also keep the "Just like me" phrases taped to the back of my badge and pull it out whenever I need to.

———

What is mindfulness meditation? Jon Kabat-Zinn, the founder of MBSR, describes it as "paying attention on purpose." Dr. David Vago, a research associate professor of psychology at the Vanderbilt Brain Institute and of psychiatry at Harvard Medical

School, defines mindfulness meditation as "a method of systematic mental training to reduce suffering and cultivate a healthy, sustainable mind." This definition resonates with me because everyone desires a healthy, sustainable mind. Why would anyone choose a mind that suffers? Suffering might seem like a strong term, but to me, it refers to anything that sparks unproductive thoughts such as worry, fear, blame, shame, guilt, or feelings of inadequacy— thoughts driven by the inner critic (a concept we will explore in depth later). When we perpetuate the habit of resistance and use distractions to avoid facing what is directly in front of us, we suffer mentally, physically, and emotionally. This is why burnout has become so prevalent. Our thinking must change. Overcoming these detrimental habits and thoughts requires time and dedication. Meditation is about clearing the storms from our minds. The mind often fixates on what's wrong or how to fix everything, instead of appreciating the blessings that are already present.

> *"My thoughts got me into worry, addiction, anxiety and*
> *I followed them for years and it got me nowhere."*
>
> **~ Client**

Your mind may be wondering, "How do we do this?" First, set the intention to break free from these mental habits. You are taking that step by reading this book. Just setting the intention to train the mind differently is the first step. It creates an opening.

Second, develop a consistent daily meditation practice to train both the heart and the mind. Mindfulness is a practice that develops over time. It is not a quick fix or an immediate solution to problems. These practices are most effective when done regularly, without expecting immediate results. Unless these methods become strong mental habits, you can't call upon them in moments of need. Attending silent retreats and working with an experienced mindfulness teacher or coach can help you develop a consistent practice. Without a mentor or coach, you are more likely to revert to old habits and excuses that hinder your practice. Having someone to hold you accountable makes it more likely that you will stick with the practice.

The benefit of attending extended seven to ten-day silent retreats is the opportunity for wisdom to arise from deep stillness. It is a profound experience that helps you understand the true nature of your mind, how it works, and the recurring themes that inhabit it. It can be painful, both emotionally and physically, but it is the only way to see where you are getting stuck in your internal narrative and in life. For example, if you spend seven days thinking about trauma from your youth, it indicates unresolved issues that need to be addressed or forgiven.

For several years, I attended ten-day silent retreats, and each time my mind was consumed with thoughts about my son, his chronic health issues, and how I might be able to fix them. This continued for five years, starting when he was seven years old. These thoughts were always in the background, suppressed to some extent to manage the daily demands of balancing work and home life. On retreat, these thoughts would surface, presenting an opportunity for me to heal this aspect of myself and lean into acceptance. Now, during silent retreats, he is no longer the dominating thought in my mind, even though his health issues remain and have been life-threatening at times. Any unresolved past experience may surface during a retreat. I consider it a gift when this happens. The experience is coming up to be resolved and healed.

One client, a successful trial lawyer, has been coaching with me for several years and recently attended his first meditation retreat. The wisdom that arose from his consistent practice and retreat allowed him to see how being bullied in middle school still impacts his life today. When he's at the gym and sees teenagers who resemble those who bullied him, he experiences an emotional response. He perceives a tone of arrogance from them, and his mind starts creating a story. These false stories keep us disconnected from others, fostering a sense of separateness that prevents deep, meaningful relationships. At the age of 60, this client now has the awareness and wisdom from his practice to see the reactivity clearly and name it for what it is. It no longer controls him.

When you hit an obstacle in your practice and don't know how to resolve it, that's when most people stop. However, working weekly with a mindfulness leadership coach can help you work through the obstacle, allowing you to grow from the experience, learn, and change your behavior based on the results.

Let's delve deeper into what this practice entails: an exploration of self-awareness. Developing a mindfulness practice allows you to cultivate an internal presence that keeps you connected to your body during moments of emotional reactivity. We train ourselves to recognize the somatic responses in our physical body when we are triggered or upset. For instance, when we're angry, we might feel heat in our body, burning ears, or a racing heart. When we're fearful, we might experience adrenaline coursing through our body, feel chilly, or notice tunnel vision. Everyone's somatic response is unique. Once you become aware of your internal responses, you can pause before reacting in a harmful or unskillful manner. Viktor Frankl, a Holocaust concentration camp survivor, explains it this way in his book, *Man's Search for Meaning*: "Forces beyond your control can take away everything you possess except one thing, your freedom to choose how you will respond to the situation. You cannot control what happens to you in life, but you can always control what you will feel and do about what happens to you."

This practice is about training the mind to move away from reacting impulsively. It allows you to see your mind clearly, free from distortions and false perceptions that lead to reactivity. You begin by training your mind in a formal discipline, which requires patience, kindness, and curiosity about the nature of your mind. It can be intimidating. Many of us are reluctant to sit and examine the nature of our thoughts. We become vulnerable when we realize how our thoughts dictate our behavior and the way we present ourselves to the world. This practice involves sitting still and observing the mind's nature. It is not about stopping thoughts but about watching them without engaging or judging. This is challenging because we are deeply conditioned to live in a mode of constant thinking. We value the thinking mind and tend to believe everything it tells us. But that is not always the case. Often, we are lost in thought. The mind is cunning that way. Even with the intention of cultivating stillness, an inner narrative often runs in the background. Studies have shown that we are lost in thought about 47% of our day, and during these times, we usually dwell on things that bother, worry, or stress us out. Rarely do we wander to thoughts of self-love, appreciation for our good fortune, or true joy. When we formally train the mind to gather and focus our attention on the present moment, we cultivate more mindfulness in life. Mindfulness helps us become less reactive and enhances our performance in every aspect of life, including leadership.

How do you begin this mental training?

1. **Set the intention**: Your intention could be to develop mindfulness, empathy, understanding, and compassion.
2. **Establish a formal practice**: Sit daily, if possible, for at least 15 minutes.
3. **Let go of distractions.**

4. **Practice non-judgment and non-striving**: Avoid judging or criticizing yourself, the experience, or even your posture. It's not a competition or a race. You are not doing it wrong.

5. **Notice everything**: Observe the flow of your breath, sensations, and temperature changes. Let everything flow in and out of your awareness.

6. **Return to your breath or the body**.

I recommend meditating for at least 15 minutes daily. In my experience, it takes about that long for the mind to begin settling. Whenever possible, I suggest longer sessions of 30 minutes or more, especially when dealing with challenging mind states like anxiety. Just as with physical training, the longer you exercise, the stronger you become. Similarly, the longer you meditate, the more stable and resilient your mind becomes.

Repetition is key. To cultivate a new habit, practice it daily. I recommend finding an experienced teacher with over 10 years of practice, who has attended regular 2-week silent retreats, to guide you, as many questions arise when beginning a meditation practice, and it's easy to get discouraged and give up. Meditation apps are a wonderful way to start if you don't have access to a teacher. However, to develop a lifelong practice, mentorship from seasoned practitioners is invaluable for skillfully navigating the mind's constructs and maintaining motivation.

For those just starting a meditation practice, I often recommend a body scan meditation. We are often disconnected from our bodies and need to learn how to reinhabit them to recognize the somatic responses resulting from our thoughts.

Below is a simple body scan practice for you to try. Please feel free to listen to my free body scan meditation on my website: https://mindfulpresence.net/body-scan-meditation/.

1. Find a comfortable posture, either lying on the floor or sitting in a chair—whichever is more accessible for you. Allow your body to relax.

2. Close your eyes if you wish or leave them open with a soft gaze.

3. Pay attention to the natural rhythm of your breathing.

4. Bring awareness to your body and notice where your body is connecting to a surface and being supported by the chair, mattress, or floor. Notice feelings of warmth or coolness in your body.

5. Begin to focus your attention on different parts of your body, scanning from your feet to your head, or from your head to your toes. There is no wrong way to do this practice.

6. For each part of the body, linger for a few moments and notice the different sensations as you focus.

7. The moment you notice that your mind has wandered, gently return your attention to the part of the body you last remember focusing on.

8. Without moving, begin to feel your toes, seeing if you can feel each toe, one at a time. Move into your legs, allowing them to feel heavy, weighted, and at peace. Sense your pelvis, abdomen, lower back, middle back, and upper back. Move to the chest, feeling it rise and fall with your breath. Feel your shoulders, sense the length of your arms down to your fingers, feeling the tips of each finger one at a time. Move to

your neck and head, softening the muscles of your face and releasing the jaw. Notice your ears and sounds. Feel the top of your head. Finally, sense your whole body from head to toe, feeling your entire body breathing in and out.

If you feel sleepy during your body scan practice, that's okay. Take a few deep breaths to reawaken and begin again. Each time you bring your wandering mind back to the body, you are doing it right.

When the body is uncomfortable, it's challenging to stay present, so we often space out. However, focusing on the body helps the mind pay attention. The body exists within awareness. Honor your body as it is in this moment. Adding respect to your meditation practice is crucial. We practice with the intention of waking up, creating an intentional life, rather than one lost in mindlessness. Seeing something clearly can set us free.

Think of your practice like going to the gym. The more you exercise, the better you feel. Each time you lift weights, you strengthen your muscles. For example, doing three sets of eight bicep curls strengthens your biceps. Similarly, in meditation, each time your mind wanders and you bring it back to the breath or body, it's like one repetition. The mind will wander repeatedly. That is the nature of the mind. Each time you bring it back, it's another repetition. This trains the mind to return to a state of balance and stillness before wandering again. Moments of stillness may last a few breaths or a full minute. Sometimes, the mind may wander for minutes or even an hour. Each day and each practice is different. If we expect the practice to be a certain way or attack our thoughts aggressively, we may become discouraged. Practicing this way reinforces clinging and striving. Instead, each time we bring the wandering mind back, it's a new beginning. Each in-breath is a new beginning, and each out-breath represents an ending. Beginning and ending. Just as your breath has a beginning and ending, every situation at work has a beginning and ending. Every difficult conversation has a beginning and ending. Every circumstance in life has a beginning and ending. Your moods begin and end. Everything is impermanent. This is what our practice teaches us. If we can live in the flow of coming and going, everything becomes easier.

If we can live in the flow of coming and going, everything becomes easier.

Perfection does not exist in meditation. If we approach training the mind as a competition, as something to achieve, it only leads to more suffering. The harder we strive, the farther off track we become. Consider the story of the student who says to the teacher, "I'm really eager to get enlightened. If I practice really hard, how long will it take?" The teacher replies, "Twenty years." This doesn't fit the student's timeline, so they ask, "Well, if I practice extra hard, how long will it take?" The teacher responds, "Thirty years." Now the student is really worried and says, "What if I sleep only a couple of hours a night and practice really, really hard the rest of the time?" The teacher says, "Forty years."

Stop trying to "win" at meditation. Instead, think of your practice the way Jon Kabat-Zinn describes it: "Meditation is like going up into your attic and emptying one box at a time." The mind works in pictures, so imagine emptying boxes of thoughts one at a time to declutter the mind. Having visual analogies like this can be helpful and give purpose to your practice. Meditation isn't about achieving anything. Let go of striving and remind yourself that each box you remove creates a new pathway in your brain to learn mindfulness.

Another technique to train your mind and escape mental chaos is to focus on an object in nature. For example, when I do this, I choose to center my attention on a patch of trees slightly turning red as fall approaches. As I remain focused on one tree, I notice birds coming and going, flying through my field of awareness, but I keep my gaze centered on the tree. I don't allow my eyes to follow the birds. I simply observe them flying in and out of my awareness. I may notice the urge to look at the birds, or I may be curious about their type. It can feel like a pull of energy, a wanting, a desire. I observe that feeling and let it float by without engaging. I stay focused on the tree while being aware of my breath moving in and out. I let the awareness of the trees and my breath fill my consciousness.

Open-eye meditation can be particularly helpful, especially when dealing with deep or painful thoughts or sleepiness. Letting your attention rest on the beauty of nature, and the impermanence of the changing seasons—like watching trees change color and leaves fall—can be grounding. It reminds you of the transient nature of all things. I encourage you to experiment with this practice during your own meditation. Imagine your thoughts are like birds flying back and forth in your field of vision. Don't engage with them. Simply observe and redirect your attention to the tree, the colors of the leaves, or whatever your chosen meditation object is.

Mindfulness: An Informal Practice

After dedicating yourself to a daily formal practice, notice how it fuels your informal practice. Informal practice involves being aware of what's happening in the moment during repetitive tasks that don't require much thought, like folding laundry, washing dishes, preparing a meal, walking the dog, or walking to your next meeting. These are moments when the mind tends to wander. Can you bring a level of awareness and attention to everyday tasks like eating a meal, brushing your teeth, putting away your groceries, or scrolling through text messages? This is mindfulness.

My favorite time to practice mindfulness is while driving. This is when my mind tends to wander the most, yet it's crucial to stay focused and not be lost in thought. Try it. When you are driving, notice if your shoulders are tense or up by your ears. Are you gripping the steering wheel tightly? Are you holding your breath or clenching your jaw? Mindfulness helps you shift your attention back to the sensation of your foot pressing on the pedal, the sensation of your hands on the steering wheel, and the color of the car in front of you. Notice how often you change the radio station or turn the radio off and on. I find that when I practice this way, I feel the pull of automaticity. I might set my intention to drive mindfully without music, yet find myself turning on the music and singing along. I do these things on autopilot, unaware until I "wake up" from the trance of automaticity and turn the music off. These moments of "waking up" are opportunities for mindfulness and becoming present again.

A method I use to stay present while driving is to send loving-kindness to the person driving in front of me by saying statements like, "May you be safe, peaceful, and happy." We will explore the heart-opening practice of loving-kindness in the next chapter. This practice invites you to accept things as they are right now, such as the car in front of you driving five miles an hour or sitting behind a driver still checking their phone after the stoplight has turned green. It doesn't mean we approve of someone's actions or have to like them.

I also use this practice in other situations, like before entering a difficult conversation or when in conflict with a client or team member at work. If we lead from the heart instead of from judgment, anger, or fear, we create a culture of acceptance, safety, and trust. All of these methods keep me in the present moment. I am training my mind from moment to moment, continually returning my attention to what is happening right now.

Through the power of training our mental faculties to cultivate qualities like intention and attention, we can create any state of mind we choose, with practice. We can create and project out into the world something positive, skillful, and wholesome, based on our intention to live with a mind resting in patience, kindness, compassion, and goodness. If we focus on those qualities and dwell in them daily, they become the nature of our experience.

Productive Multitasking Is a Myth

In today's world, where multitasking is rampant, people often juggle multiple tasks at once in an attempt to accomplish more. This leaves the mind feeling unsteady and scattered, counterproductive to the goal of creating a healthy, sustainable mind. Multitasking derails us from establishing and committing to a lifelong practice of mental training. Dr. Amishi Jha, professor of psychology at the University of Miami and Director and co-founder of Contemplative Neuroscience for the Mindfulness Research and Practice Initiative, states that multitasking is a myth. It's actually mental switching in the mind. Dr. Jha's research shows that when we multitask, it takes time to get back on track with the original task. Multitasking fatigues the brain, leading to more mistakes. Our brains respond as if we stayed up all night. According to a University of California, Irvine study, "it takes an average of 23 minutes and 15 seconds to get back to the task." Clearly, multitasking is unproductive and leads to burnout, making us feel like we have nothing left to give.

In some cultures, multitasking is worn like a badge of honor. Many of my clients boast, "I am great at multitasking!" They think it's a sought-after skill, but it only exhausts the mind and creates more confusion. It scatters our focus and increases errors. Training the mind to flit from one thing to the next, or constantly seeking distractions, harms performance. We respond slower to situations requiring full attention and take time to reengage with tasks or conversations. Multitasking is the antithesis of mindfulness.

Leaders need access to their working memory to solve problems, create presentations, make investment recommendations, and fully listen to colleagues sharing valuable insights. Working memory is tied to our attention, which degrades when we multitask, leading to costly mistakes like making a million-dollar error in a financial trade. Moreover, a mind constantly seeking external pleasure or calm is not at ease. As humans, we all want to feel good, but our minds often search for external ways to achieve this instead of turning inward.

Instead of multitasking, we can practice mindful tasking. Intentionally notice when you shift from one task to another and become aware of how it feels in your body. For example, notice when you switch from writing an email to checking your phone, even when not expecting a text. What does that feel like? It might feel like restlessness, adrenaline, or something else. Be mindful of switching from tasks requiring deep concentration to something like scrolling the Internet. Is it a distraction? Are you stuck or bored? What motivates the desire to switch to something less intense?

By observing your habits and patterns, you can become aware of them rather than being driven by automaticity. Sometimes multitasking is necessary. For example, financial traders must multitask, executing multiple trades while following current markets on Bloomberg screens and listening to the trading floor's activity and what might affect their trades. Trading rooms are hubs of activity in any investment house. Knowing I caution against multitasking, traders ask what to do if their job requires it. If this applies to you, notice the physical effects on your body while multitasking and turn your awareness to these sensations throughout the day. Make meditation a priority after work to focus and concentrate the mind in the present moment, avoiding carrying multitasking mode into the evening. At work, give the mind time to settle and stabilize between switching tasks by pausing for three deep breaths, counting to 10 before engaging in the next task, or scanning your body: head, arms, torso, legs, and feet, and then move to the next task or meeting.

With training, a leader can move from one meeting to the next with clarity and full attention, unaffected by the prior meeting. Their mind fully switches to the new task or meeting, remaining fully engaged.

When possible, use time blocking in your schedule. If overwhelmed with your task list, divide each hour into 15-minute increments and assign tasks to each part: reply to emails, organize presentations, edit reports, or write performance reviews. This way, you may switch tasks, but you will be productive, move through your to-do list, and support your mind to regain clarity.

LOVING KINDNESS PRACTICE

Elaine's Story

As a female leader in a male-dominated industry, I dealt with a lot of stress and frustration. I credit my mindfulness practice with helping me through the last several years, during which I stopped accepting bad behavior and started pushing for change. Through mindfulness, I gained clarity and confidence that allowed me to face challenges head-on. I stopped letting negativity and bad behavior bring me down and instead used it to fuel my drive for change. The calm confidence I gained from my practice and trainings made me more effective.

By practicing mindfulness, I have become a better leader, a less emotional investor, and a less stressed coworker, friend, and family member. My mindfulness practice has touched all facets of my life, giving me the tools to "take it down a notch" when needed. Just the other day, as I was juggling prep for a board meeting, mentoring at a nonprofit, dealing with a personnel situation, and helping a coworker—all while preparing for a graduation party—the stress level was reaching a boiling point. I sat in my car in the Target parking lot and, instead of screaming (my old default), I did a short meditation that allowed me to put everything in perspective. *A little loving-kindness practice can go a long way* in pulling myself out of the clouds and into the calmness and control I needed to not just juggle but to manage the situations, prioritize, and be an effective and pleasant leader, organizer, and person.

—● ◖—

"Love is the ultimate and the highest goal to which man can aspire…. The salvation of man is through love and in love."

~ Viktor Frankl

Loving-kindness meditation is an excellent way to shift away from a self-critical mind that either wants to know everything or thinks it knows everything. It fosters an attitude of acceptance and kindness towards ourselves and others. In my opinion, loving-kindness meditation is a gold-standard leadership strategy for increasing resilience, fostering positive emotions, and enhancing empathy while counteracting stress and burnout.

I find that loving-kindness and compassion are sometimes used interchangeably, but they are distinct. Loving-kindness is a practice that plants the seeds of befriending ourselves and others with love and kindness. It's about caring and listening with an open heart, free from judgment. It cultivates a generous heart for the well-being and happiness of others and ourselves. It counteracts deep internal mental forces like judgment, criticism, fear, and harm.

Compassion, on the other hand, is about turning toward suffering without taking on the suffering of others and making it our own. Christina Feldman, author of *Boundless Heart*, says, "Compassion is not a state or an emotion but an understanding. It is an understanding rooted in the classroom of our lives and hearts and in a genuine and honest investigation of our own relationship to pain and to suffering." She describes compassion as the cultivation of friendliness towards all living beings, including oneself. This doesn't mean you have to like, agree with, approve of others or even like the patterns within yourself. It means learning to receive whatever arises in the moment with presence. We can be aware of hatred and aversion without dwelling on them, so we don't add to their energy. The cultivation of compassion is like a powerful medicine. It dissolves the toxins of resentment, hatred, rage, and unhealthy competitiveness. Its blessings are many, as it aids concentration and frees the mind from aversion.

The mind thrives on a steady diet of love and kindness. Unfortunately, most of us do not spend much of our day treating ourselves kindly in our minds. My first in-depth experience with loving-kindness practice was on a seven-day silent retreat with Sharon Salzberg and Oren Jay Sofer at Insight Meditation Center in Barre, MA, almost ten years ago. During this retreat, I deeply immersed myself in cultivating kindness toward myself and others over seven days. My heart opened. I felt lighter, happier, and more at ease. I began to practice infusing my attention with care and compassion daily, similar to a parent attending to a young child, saying to myself, "I honor this. I give myself permission to feel what I feel." It was transformational. My heart softened, and I rested in that inner space of ease and happiness for many months. When you are centered in your heart, everything flows in life.

One of the practices during that retreat was to do walking meditation using the loving-kindness phrases we were exploring in meditation that week. My phrases were "May I be safe and protected. May I be happy. May I be healthy."

It was suggested to those of us in attendance that we each assign a word from our loving-kindness phrases to each footfall. I chose the words safe, happy, and healthy. The instruction was to repeat this over and over again as we walked, assigning a word to each step, each footfall:

Safe. Happy. Healthy.

Safe. Happy. Healthy.

As we walked, we were encouraged to send loving-kindness to anything we came across on our path—trees, animals, a person driving by, a caterpillar. On my walk, I came across a farm with cows. As I stood in front of the cows, sending them loving-kindness for several minutes—"May you be safe and protected, may you be healthy, may you be happy"—an enormous amount of emotion welled up inside me. I felt deeply connected with these animals before me. At that point, I thought to myself: "Oh my goodness, I'm going crazy. I am talking to cows." Yet, every day on my walk, I looked for the cows and felt disappointed when they weren't there. So, I made that part of my practice. I recognized 'disappointment' when the cows were absent, made a mental note of it, and continued my walk. This is meditation: to notice *everything*.

The lesson for me in this practice was understanding deeply that how we cultivate our hearts affects every aspect of our lives. It influences how we perceive every human being, nature, and the world at large. If our hearts are always inclined towards loving-kindness, there's no room for hatred, bitterness, ill will, or resentment to arise.

Shifting our attention to loving-kindness is a powerful way to "lighten our load" and redirect our minds away from lack, criticism and unwholesome thoughts; thoughts like believing that things will never change or that life is hard. It also helps to slow us down. For me, I feel less urgency when I am centered in my heart. I am kinder to myself and everyone around me. No matter where we begin, stepping into a practice of meditation lightens our burden by shifting our focus. By cultivating wise attention, we see beyond limitations, freeing our minds and easing our load.

No matter where we begin, stepping into a practice of meditation lightens our burden by shifting our focus. By cultivating wise attention, we see beyond limitations, freeing our minds and easing our load.

Loving-kindness practice helps shift us from an "I, me, mine" perspective to a "we" way of being. It engages the default mode network of the brain, which is responsible for our personal narrative. This practice can be directed towards yourself, those you care about, perceived enemies, and all beings everywhere. Start with what feels comfortable, accepting thoughts and feelings as they arise during meditation. Practicing loving-kindness sets the intention to soften the heart, training it to be receptive and stretching the mind beyond its tendency to contract. It invites us to soften into the moment, increasing our capacity for patience and reducing reactivity. Wisdom can arise, leading to better choices and a sense of peace. It creates an upward spiral, making more space in our lives and allowing teachings to flow in and guide us to act skillfully.

Sometimes loving-kindness practice is the only way to cope with difficult situations, like losing a loved one or receiving a challenging medical diagnosis. It's an incredibly powerful practice. You don't have to be good at it, and honestly, you can't do it wrong.

I invite you to experiment with this practice using the following phrases:

- May I be happy.
- May I be healthy.
- May I be peaceful.
- May I accept things as they are.
- May my mind and heart awaken.
- May I be free.

If you prefer, you can use the phrase "I wish" for myself to be well and happy or "I wish" for you to be well and happy. Sharon Salzberg teaches that wishing this for another person is like wishing them a happy birthday.

Feel free to modify the phrases in any way that resonates with you, or create your own. You can use just two or three phrases if that works better for you. Begin by calling to mind an image of yourself and silently repeat the phrases three to four times, or longer if time permits. The more you practice, the better you will feel. Imagine each phrase moving through every cell of your body like a soothing balm. Maintain an attitude of kindness towards yourself, regardless of what you are experiencing in the moment. If the phrases feel difficult to connect with or mechanical in nature, remember that the most important aspect is your intention to awaken the heart.

Next, repeat the phrases while calling to mind an image of someone you care about and would like to send these phrases to. Repeat the phrases three to four times or more. Then, imagine sending them to someone you have difficulty with, hold resentment towards, or do not feel at peace with—a perceived enemy. Visualize them sitting next to you or imagine their image. Lastly, send the phrases out to all beings everywhere. You can image an image of the world or a globe. Allow space between the phrases to pause and reflect. Notice if you are rushing through the phrases. Be aware of any somatic responses in the body and notice what you feel.

It can be easier to focus on loving-kindness phrases for those we care about, such as close friends and family. However, it can be more challenging to extend loving-kindness towards those who trigger us or have hurt us. Mindfulness is a powerful tool for acknowledging and releasing any hurt, resentment, or ill will we may hold towards others. Instead, try sending love to those who cause you distress or harm. Holding onto anger, hurt, and resentment only harms you. It burns like a fire, preventing you from experiencing overall well-being, happiness, and ease in your life. It disrupts the natural flow of giving and receiving all things. When you release the negative emotions you hold towards others, you shift your energy and vibration, creating more harmony and positivity within yourself, which in turn attracts more of the same. Love has the power to heal and transform even the most challenging situations. Commit to sending love to those who bother and challenge you, and observe the impact it has on your health, wealth, and overall happiness.

"If we are angry at many people, we start to live in a climate of hate. People will get angry at us in return. If we cultivate love, it returns to us. It's simply how the law works in our lives."

~ Jack Kornfield

Practice loving-kindness meditation once a day for 15 minutes, four or five times a week. Set a timer for 15 minutes and sit quietly, repeating the phrases silently to yourself. Train your mind to return to the phrases whenever it wanders. Invite these phrases into your mind first thing in the morning, before you get out of bed, and at the end of your day. It's a wonderful way to bookend your day with kindness and compassion. Or, start and/or end your daily meditation practice with loving-kindness.

There are many phrases you can use in your practice. In my personal practice, I use the following:

- May I be well and happy.
- May I know my own goodness.
- May whatever covers my heart be released.

You don't have to know what covers your heart. The intention is to be free from whatever may be guarding or blocking your heart.

- May I live with an open heart.

Incorporate loving-kindness practice into your day to cultivate love and attract experiences filled with love. Do this especially when you notice you are caught in self-judgment. It only takes a few minutes and can be hugely effective over time. We can train ourselves to be compassionate; it just takes practice. Recent research studies show that brain circuits detecting emotions change in people who have been practicing compassion meditation. We have the ability to change our entire outlook—we just need to be willing to make it a priority.

PROCESSING EMOTIONS

The Ability to Manage Emotions Makes us Stronger and Less Reactive Leaders

Marie's Story - Emotions

The addition of a mindfulness practice has made me a better leader. Working in the investment industry, which is highly stressful and charged with emotion, coupled with my naturally empathetic and emotionally driven personality, presents both positives and negatives when investing and leading. The level of control and calm I can now reach since incorporating mindfulness has allowed me to make better decisions, diffuse situations, and cut through the emotion to act on the facts. Mindfulness and emotional intelligence training have enhanced my self-awareness, resulting in a more thoughtful and less stressed self.

——— ——

"When a person has a reaction to something in their environment, there's a 90-second chemical process that happens

in the body; after that, any remaining emotional response is just the person choosing to stay in that emotional loop."

~ Dr. Jill Bolte Taylor,
Harvard-trained neuroscientist,
author of ***My Stroke of Insight***

In my experience, one of the ways to maintain a long-lasting practice is by working with your emotions. Sometimes it is very difficult to sit with the intensity of emotions held in the body and mind. Being aware of your emotions affects how you lead and supports your ability to choose how you participate in conversations and in life. When you name your emotions and identify their

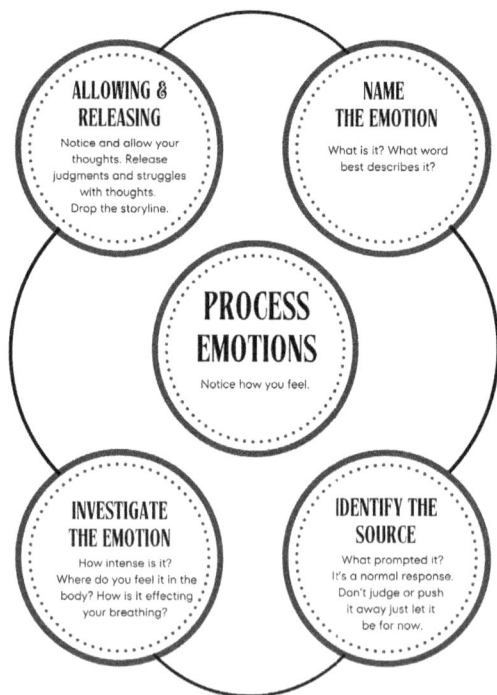

ALLOWING & RELEASING
Notice and allow your thoughts. Release judgments and struggles with thoughts. Drop the storyline.

NAME THE EMOTION
What is it? What word best describes it?

PROCESS EMOTIONS
Notice how you feel.

INVESTIGATE THE EMOTION
How intense is it? Where do you feel it in the body? How is it effecting your breathing?

IDENTIFY THE SOURCE
What prompted it? It's a normal response. Don't judge or push it away just let it be for now.

components, it helps you self-regulate. This creates perspective and softens the emotion, releasing its charge over you. Emotions simply want your attention. With mindfulness, you can develop your capacity to identify and regulate emotions. In doing so, you change your behavior, leading to different results.

How to process emotions:

1. Name the emotion

What is it? Use whatever word best describes it. Be factual. Do you feel fear, anger, sadness, grief, joy, discontentment, loneliness, or guilt? If it's difficult to determine the exact emotion, label it with a word like 'overwhelm' or 'upset' if that seems appropriate. Sometimes we are caught in reactivity and cannot discern what emotion is occurring. It can be helpful to use a different word than one that habitually comes to mind. For example, "overwhelmed" is a common word I hear often when guiding others in this process. To gain more clarity, ask yourself: What is at the root of overwhelm? Is it sadness, unhappiness, despair, hurt, or discouragement? There are many descriptive words for each of the five main emotions. See if you can find a word that clearly describes what you are feeling.

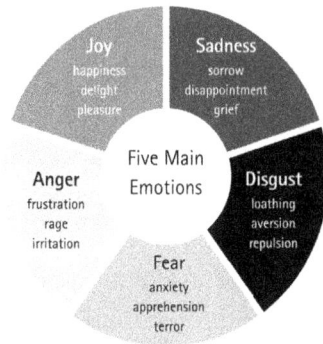

2. Identify the Source

Where did this emotion come from? What prompted it? Was it a conversation you had with someone, or did you receive an upsetting performance review? Or is it an old emotion resurfacing from an event years ago or from the way you were raised? Be skillful and avoid judging the experience. Gently acknowledge what caused this emotion to arise. Let it be for now.

3. Investigate the Emotion

Where are you feeling the emotion in your body? Name the location. Are you feeling it in the head, jaw, chest, heart, stomach, back, or somewhere else? Is it fleeting or does it remain over time? As you pay attention to the emotion, notice how it affects your breathing. Is your breathing short or shallow? Is it long or deep? Is it jittery or jagged? Is it rapid or slow?

Our bodies hold everything. Your body holds all the emotions and experiences you encounter in life, both big traumas and little traumas. Dr. Bessel van der Kolk, an expert on trauma and author of *The Body Keeps the Score*, explains through science how trauma reshapes the body and brain, and how emotional regulation is critical in managing the effects of trauma.

> *"Trauma interferes with the brain circuits that involve focusing, flexibility, and being able to stay in emotional control. Neuroscience research has shown that traumatized individuals are prone to activate brain areas involved in fear perception, and to have deficits in the areas involved in filtering out relevant from irrelevant information, as well as in the perception of bodily sensations. These changes do not occur in the rational part of the brain."*
>
> ~ Dr. Bessel van der Kolk

I have come to understand that I hold emotions in my stomach. Whenever I have a strong emotional response, I feel it there. It's like a 'gut' felt sense reacting to what I'm experiencing. Some clients also report feeling their emotional responses in their stomachs, while others feel it in their head, neck, chest, or back. Notice where your body holds your emotions. When you can identify what you are feeling, you gain control over yourself. This is self-leadership. It enables you to stay on task better, engage fully with others, and appreciate life more deeply.

> **When you can identify what you are feeling, you gain control of yourself. This is self-leadership. It allows you to stay on task better, engage fully with others, and appreciate life more deeply.**

Notice how the emotion is affecting your physical body. What do you feel physically? Every emotion has a certain tone to it. Anger may feel fiery and hot, like fire burning through your veins. Sadness may feel heavy and weighted, perhaps like depression. Joy may feel light and tingly. Observe the tone or physical sensations of the experience. Do you feel pulsing, pressure, heaviness, lightness, emptiness, spaciousness, dizziness, gripping, or something else? Identify the sensations and note them silently to yourself as you witness them rising.

4. Allowing and Releasing

As you rest in the sensations that the emotion is producing, practice silently saying to yourself "allowing and accepting" as you breathe in and out. Release any storyline or attachment to the emotion. You are allowing the emotions to be processed in the physical container of the body and accepting them as they are. The intensity of the emotion may become stronger as you sit with it. You may feel the urge to jump out of your seat to avoid what you are feeling. You might experience sweating, nausea, dizziness—anything can arise. The energy of what has been suppressed and held back will manifest when you soften. It comes to the surface to clear out. Bear with it without contracting, and let the waves of energy roll through you with compassion. Grasp nothing and reject nothing.

> "Feel it, the thing that you don't want to feel. Feel it and be free."
>
> ~ Nayyirah Waheed

Recognize that these experiences are impermanent. They will come and go. All physical and mental states are fleeting by nature. Sometimes they linger longer than we would like, but your role as the meditator is to sit with the intensity of what arises. As you do so, you realize that everything is changing and fluid, and you have a choice in how you respond. Irritation, for example, is just irritation; there's no need to make more of it. One of my teachers describes emotions as a forest fire. A forest fire rages out of control as long as it has trees, grass, and brush to feed on. Once everything is burned away, the fire dies out because it has nothing left to fuel it. Our emotions work similarly. When we continue to fuel our emotions with negative thoughts, they rage out of control. Our human nature is to keep returning to the things that bother us, keeping us stuck in the emotional response to the thought. This is the root of reactivity and suffering. To move away from suffering, refrain from focusing on the emotional pain of the past and instead notice your present moment awareness of the emotion as it arises now. Once you stop feeding the emotion with self-limiting beliefs, internal stories, distortions, and perceptions that may not be true, it eventually dissipates, freeing you from internal suffering. Chaos, confusion, struggle, and burnout do not have to be permanent ways of life. Freedom from these deeply rooted habit patterns is possible.

Continually train your mind to return to awareness of the body. Allow the sensations to process naturally without interference, resistance, or avoidance. Many people aren't taught or permitted to feel their emotions. Often, we are conditioned to numb ourselves and avoid our feelings. My teacher, Oren Jay Sofer, discusses this in his book *Say What You Mean*. He explains, "When we are experiencing a strong emotion, it tells us something is important to us. If there is an emotion, something matters. Emotions are primary ways the body-mind sends signals about our needs." It's essential to understand and pay attention to our emotions. Don't deny or push them away. Oren uses the analogy of a smoke alarm going off in your home. You wouldn't ignore it; you would address it immediately. Our emotions deserve the same attention. Honor them, respect them, listen to them. Invite them in and allow the full expression of the emotions to move through you. Remember, it will only take 90 seconds, according to Dr. Jill Bolte Taylor.

Once the physical response to the emotion has subsided, we train our minds to return to the meditation object of our choice. This may be the breath, the body, a physical reference point like your hands or feet, or a word or phrase. A phrase that I often return to is "May I be at ease." It serves as a reminder to return to the stillness and quiet within, moving away from the turbulent mind.

If you are experiencing an internal struggle and cannot sit with what is happening, it's important to pay attention. It's signaling that something really matters to you. Joseph Goldstein, one of the early pioneers of bringing meditation teachings to the West and author of *Mindfulness: A Practical Guide to Awakening*, teaches that "feelings of struggle can become very useful feedback. They are always telling us that something is going on that we're not accepting, not opening to. Because if we were accepting it, we wouldn't be struggling." Struggle can arise from anything: restlessness, pain, sleepiness, an active mind, a difficult situation, lack of motivation to practice, or something else. If the struggle stems from a proliferation of thoughts, examine "your" internal story honestly. Where are you caught in a struggle with yourself? Are you making whatever is happening now all about you? Could there be another way to view it?

When we practice in this way, being aware of struggle, we become strong leaders and influencers in our lives. We learn to reflect, investigate, and be curious, inviting everything in without trying to figure it all out immediately. We don't react blindly or habitually, nor do we make excuses outside of ourselves to deflect our involvement in the experience. This practice trains us to be more self-aware, emotionally regulated, mentally flexible, and adaptable. Whether you are a leader in a corporation, a school, or a rock star mom leading your family, your practice becomes who you are. You develop deeper empathy and maintain a positive outlook even in difficult circumstances. You can create meaningful change.

Inviting in struggle is an interesting way to investigate it. A way to practice this is to "welcome" your experience of struggle. The deeply introspective Rumi poem, "The Guest House," epitomizes this practice.

> This being human is a guest house.
> Every morning a new arrival.
>
> A joy, a depression, a meanness,
> some momentary awareness comes
> as an unexpected visitor.

Welcome and entertain them all!
Even if they're a crowd of sorrows,
who violently sweep your house
empty of its furniture,
still, treat each guest honorably.
He may be clearing you out
for some new delight.

The dark thought, the shame, the malice,
meet them at the door laughing,
and invite them in.

Be grateful for whoever comes,
because each has been sent
as a guide from beyond.

When the mind is overcome by strong emotions, such as anger, shame, loathing, or disgust, invite them in. Say "welcome" to them. They are guests in your home, your internal home, your mind. Be open to the idea that these difficult situations are opportunities for growth. Treat them kindly. Just like guests in your home, thoughts, emotions, and experiences don't stay forever. They come and they go. When we cling to them, they linger. I invite you to try this in your practice. When you're sitting in silence and you notice a disturbing thought, rumination, or obsession arriving, silently say "welcome." You can also practice this actively during your day at work or in moments when you notice you are triggered and something unpleasant arises. Say "welcome" out loud or silently to yourself. By doing this, you remind yourself to invite in your experience as it is happening rather than resisting it or making excuses about it. It takes much more energy to avoid, resist, or run away from experiences than to feel them. Suppression doesn't work either.

Suppression only keeps you stuck in the cycle of suffering and, eventually, emotions will erupt like a volcano.

> *"Suppression is like driftnet fishing. In the effort to target certain negative emotions, suppression ends up catching everything in its path. So we stuff down not only the unwanted emotions, but also access to feelings we do want such as joy, warmth, affection, and connection to others."*
>
> ~ Leah Weiss, PhD.

The burdens you carry in life can weigh heavily on your mind and may frequently appear during meditation when you are still. Your practice is a reminder to put those burdens down, to let go, and to release all that is hindering your mind for the duration of your practice. Meditation is not about trying to solve your problems, create clarity, or think about anything specific. It's a non-doing practice. It's about just *being*.

Mindfully Taming the Inner Critic

How to Work with the Voice In Your Head

Jacqueline's Story

How has this practice and private coaching made a difference in my life and changed my relationships? Mindfulness practice in its entirety has transformed my life. I am not sure if I will ever be able to fully verbalize how this practice has saved me. I am grateful every day for Christine and her continued teaching and support. Before meeting Christine and immersing myself in the practice, I was vulnerable, lost, and misunderstood. I struggled with anxiety, and at times it was debilitating. I could not start my day without dry heaving. It was mentally challenging, and I struggled to understand why something was happening to me. Through practice and teachings, I realized I was stuck in a paradigm that was trapping and sabotaging me. Things just happen. I was creating a narrative in my head that didn't exist. I was able to process past trauma and events that were essentially holding me back. It is not easy work. Becoming uncomfortable with emotions is key to moving forward. There were times when I wanted to stop in the session. I knew I could not stop and break the processing. Sitting with the emotions allows all parts to fully heal.

I am comfortable with the unknown now. Uncertainty used to scare me. I know that it's the path to the future, and I trust it will guide me through my life journey. I find myself with a greater appreciation for my loved ones. There were times my core relationships were strained, and I harbored guilt. Through boundary setting and communication techniques, I was able to repair some of the strain.

The practice is not a Band-Aid, but a journey someone has to be ready to take. It can be hard when someone is not ready to accept that journey, but radiating love and kindness their way is the only remedy.

——— ——

"Instead of constantly trying to pacify our Inner Critic, it can help to just label it for what it is, an entrenched mental habit of judging ourselves harshly and mostly without reason, but with mindfulness we can create some distance from it."

~ Dr. Mark Bertin

Each of us has an inner critic, a voice in our head that constantly points out what we should be doing, thinking, and feeling. It is part of who we are, but it doesn't have to dominate the conversation. Mindfulness practice helps us control the tendency of the inner critic to fuel a narrative—the silent conversation in your mind, often unconscious—of failure and blame, by redirecting our critical faculties towards taking a clearer, more comprehensive view of any situation. By short-circuiting the self-defeating narratives that arise in the face of challenges and keep us clouded, mindfulness practice trains our minds to be more flexible.

Many of my clients express the deep inner conflict they have with the voice in their heads. This narrative is more clearly heard when we are sitting in silence, training the mind, and paying attention to the present moment. What many notice are certain beliefs, recurring thoughts, and stories they tell themselves that keep appearing and often have an underlying theme of low self-worth. Phrases like, "They don't like me," or "I have to take care of others before myself," or "Nobody understands me." You may even say, "I'm the worst meditator!" I hear that one often. A phrase Jon Kabat-Zinn wrote years ago that stays fresh in my mind is: "If you have a body and you're breathing, you can meditate." In other words, anyone can meditate, even if they have a strong inner critic.

The following are some narratives that clients have shared with me over the years. Perhaps you can relate to some of these:

- Maybe I'm not that good and I pulled the wool over everyone's eyes.
- Everything is my fault.
- My anxiety is causing me to underperform at work.
- Why can't I make a decision?
- I don't know what I am doing.
- I did this to myself. I deserve this.
- I should have more willpower.
- I'm doing everything wrong.
- I don't feel heard.

Such repetitive loops spin around and around in the mind with tremendous power, until we are forced to become aware of them. Most people struggle to silence the voice in their head and find they can't maintain relationships at work, lead authentically, or connect wholeheartedly until they drop their self-limiting narrative. Statements like these lack self-compassion and make you feel there is something wrong with you, perpetuating feelings of separation, isolation, and competition. This mindset may even lead to procrastination or avoiding aspects of leadership that require courage, determination, or immediate decisions. Indecisiveness is frequently rooted in fear stemming from a lack of self-worth or self-esteem fueled by the inner critic.

What exactly is the inner critic, and how do you tame it? It's a dysfunctional attitude fueled by rumination and self-limiting thoughts or beliefs. It's a draining mental pattern, usually filled with self-judgment and loathing, which can lead to burnout. Often, it operates on autopilot. Sometimes we aren't even aware of the critic's voice running in the background of our minds throughout the day. It can be very sneaky. Self-critical thinking sounds like: "I'll never be happy," "Why do these things always happen to me?" "Why do I keep responding this way?" "I don't believe in myself," "What if I am rejected?" It can also appear when we begin a statement with "I should." Statements like "I should exercise more," "I should eat better," "I should stop drinking," "I should visit my parents more," "I should quit my job," "I should ask for a raise," etc., do not help. Such statements make you question yourself and generally result in feeling inadequate or like you're not enough. They can hold you back from reaching your potential and taking actions in your best interest.

The good news is that mindfulness targets our narrative self and decreases mind wandering. Practicing mindfulness allows you to put a pause between the voice in your head and the present moment, helping you to question your thinking rather than your-self. When we pause and become aware of this deeply entrenched mental habit, we can redirect our minds towards something more useful, wholesome, and beneficial. This could be joy, gratitude, appreciation, or loving-kindness towards yourself or others. It might involve appreciating something good in your life or recon-necting with the awareness of your body, recognizing that without this body, you wouldn't be having the experiences you are having. Numerous research studies have shown that through mindfulness practice, activity in the cortical midline structures—the part of the brain related to your personal narrative—decreases; meanwhile, activity in the insula—the part of the brain related to subjective and body awareness—increases.

> **Practicing mindfulness allows you to put a pause
> between the voice in your head and the present
> moment, helping you question your *thinking* rather
> than *yourself*.**

Now, you may be thinking, "What is the best way to target the inner critic?" The truth is, all mindfulness practices can target the inner critic, but some methods might work better for certain indi-viduals. In my experience, loving-kindness meditation has been the most effective practice for taming my inner critic. Love counteracts fear, and often the inner critic is rooted in fear. Use phrases such as, "May I be kind to myself in this moment. This is just a moment of judgment or criticism." Acknowledging the voice is crucial for becoming aware of it. If you can identify what triggered it (a tough conversation, a disappointment, or a perceived failure) and recog-nize what you feel emotionally (anger, hurt, or jealousy), it allows you to see the truth and weakens its grip on you.

Another effective method is making a silent note in the mind, like, "Ah, there it is again." When you can say lightly, "There's that story, that narrative. 'I see you,'" it loosens the inner critic's hold on you. Just seeing it clearly in the moment and acknowledging it can be enough to soften it. At that moment, shift your mind towards something more wholesome, like loving-kindness or what brings you joy. The key is to see it clearly when it begins and then redirect your mind away from it so you're not fueling it and giving it energy by focusing on it. You are not feeding the critic with more stories, self-limiting beliefs, or judgments. If you start blaming or defending, you engage the critic again. Acknowledge it immediately to stop the voice in your head as soon as it begins. Even saying "STOP" in a firm inner voice can disrupt the pattern. You have a choice: remain stuck in the pattern or break free. Leading from your inner critic daily makes you a less effective leader. An effective leader can provide constructive feedback and recognize how the inner critic operates in others at work. If you can't see the critic in yourself, it's hard to see it in others. Keeping the critic at bay allows you to connect with others, show empathy, and lead from your true, authentic self.

One client of mine, Lori, a senior project manager, was preparing for her year-end review and was anxious about receiving feedback from her boss, who was not skilled at giving clear feedback. Because the feedback Lori received was vague—"You're not being effective"—she wasn't sure how to improve. As a result, she became defensive and tried to demonstrate all the ways she was being effective. Lori was caught in an internal story that she would receive a bad review because of the feedback she was receiving. By working with Lori's inner critic, addressing fear-based thinking, and using compassion practices, she transformed the relationship. We worked together weekly for four months, and her review was outstanding. As a result of her coaching, she also developed an unexpected friendship with her boss. Her responses to her boss were fueled by her inner critic, ego, and fear-based thinking. None of it was true!

The goal is to distance yourself from the inner critic. The critic is just a reaction to something. With mindfulness, you're hearing the voice but not identifying with it. You create space between yourself and the critic. Once you become skilled at noticing the inner critic and turning away from it, rather than letting it control your mind and actions, you can begin to notice the inner critic in others. This provides insight into why others might behave in certain ways— they may be driven by their insecurities sparked by their inner critic.

When you begin a meditation practice, you may notice that your inner critic becomes louder and more dominant when feelings of failure, insecurity, guilt, or embarrassment arise. Here are some techniques to address it in the moment:

1. **Don't push it away or let it undermine you**. Remember, you can't stop thoughts by forcing them away. Instead, stop fueling the critic with more stories and invite humor. Humor is a powerful way to derail the inner critic. Think of a funny story, a sitcom character, a skit from *Saturday Night Live*, or anything that makes you laugh. It's impossible to hold a negative thought in your mind when focused on humor and positivity.

2. **Spread goodwill**. When you start to feel bad about yourself, immediately text or call someone to tell them how much you appreciate them or share something you love about them. Do this with the genuine intention of doing something good for someone else, not just to make yourself feel better. Try this and see for yourself if it creates more well-being.

3. **Ask yourself, "Is this true? Is it REALLY true? What if it wasn't true?"** What does that feel like? Are you making it true to fuel the fire of thought and feel justified? Stop and pivot to one of your positive qualities that build inner strength. Hold the image of that quality in your mind: "I am an intentional leader." "I am in charge of my thoughts." "I am enough."

Avoid giving energy and time to the negative aspects of your inner critic that focus on the past—failures, hurts, and traumas. I understand everyone has experienced these things. Your focus should be on growth and cultivating a growth mindset. You can create something better by changing your thoughts and refusing to give power to your inner critic, regardless of where you are or where you've been in life.

THE LADDER OF INFERENCE

Joshua's Story

On some levels, I think I was a very good leader in the law firm. I never asked for more than I was willing to do myself. I cared deeply and was very loyal to my team. I gave credit openly whenever it was due. I rewarded good work and instilled a high standard for our work, making them better lawyers.

But I often succumbed to the pressures of the job. It was extraordinarily demanding, with more work than could be done in a day, a week, a month, or a year. It was never-ending and very challenging. We handled some of the most complex litigations in the country, going up against some of the best lawyers, with highly sophisticated and demanding clients. The pressure was constant to turn out superior products and find ways to win. As a partner in the law firm, I was also responsible for bringing in work to feed the team and running my larger practice group.

A common consequence of that pressure was letting moments unduly influence my behavior. I never yelled or screamed, but my impatience was always present. I created a pure meritocracy without considering the consequences of that environment on those affected by it. There were winners and losers all the time, and I did little to cushion the blows. I demanded so much of myself and was impatient when others did not do the same, as unfair or unrealistic as that may have been. While I never lost my temper, it was always just below the surface, and my team was surely aware of that. As one associate put it, I was the "dad" in the room, but I am sure I was an extremely demanding dad that took no excuses.

So how has that changed? In almost every way imaginable. It started with apologies to those I most impacted. As a result of our work, I have had enough time and space to see myself, my thoughts, and my actions more objectively. I have had enough time and space to acknowledge my failures and not be afraid of them. That has allowed me to acknowledge the times where my behavior resulted in harm or at least a negative impact, and to acknowledge that to the people I affected. Needless to say, that process has been highly beneficial for all involved.

In terms of my daily interactions, my practice has given me the space to recognize my thoughts as something separate from myself and process them before I was high up the ladder of reactivity and acted on them. It has allowed me to recognize conditioned responses for what they are and how existing conditions affect my impulse to act. I am far from perfect—nirvana will not be achieved in this lifetime—but I am much more capable of looking at my actions through the prism of the recipient of those actions and modifying my behavior accordingly. I am, without question, kinder, more patient, and a better listener.

That shows up in small ways all the time. I am more inclined to make requests rather than demands and to allow for more flexible deadlines. I have been able to let things go where before I had to correct them. I problem-solve from a more relaxed perspective, trying better to understand all sides to achieve the best results. I try to listen more and speak less.

It has also impacted my relationship with other leaders in the firm. Before, I often fed the wrong wolf. I thought I wanted power to achieve other goals and desired power for the recognition and approval that came with it. Now, I seek out opportunities that are meaningful to me and helpful to others. For instance, I now run our trial academy for our associates, and my focus is on creating a positive, non-judgmental environment—something I would not have been capable of even thinking about, let alone doing, just a few years ago.

The Ladder of Inference was first introduced in 1970 by Chris Argyris, a business theorist and author associated with Harvard Business School. This tool helps us understand how we make decisions by outlining the mental steps from observation, through interpretation, to assumptions and actions based on those assumptions. Mindfulness allows you to see how you are climbing "The Ladder of Inference" in terms of your internal story and the emotions you are experiencing. I find it helpful to remember to come back down the ladder when caught in reactivity. During a difficult situation or experience, it may be challenging to recall the ladder. I suggest my clients print it out to pin to their desk, keep in their calendar, or write it out themselves. Come back down the ladder to observe the data, the facts of what is happening in the moment. Repetition is key to learning this process.

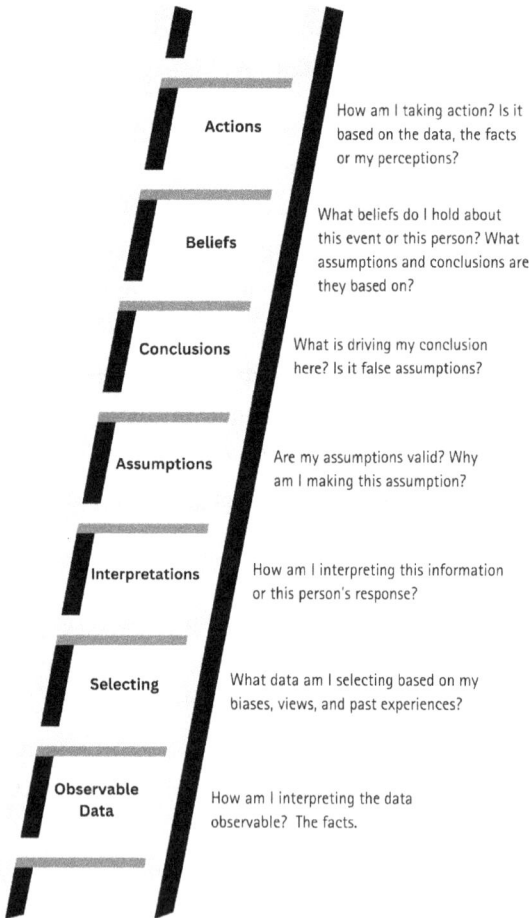

Actions — How am I taking action? Is it based on the data, the facts or my perceptions?

Beliefs — What beliefs do I hold about this event or this person? What assumptions and conclusions are they based on?

Conclusions — What is driving my conclusion here? Is it false assumptions?

Assumptions — Are my assumptions valid? Why am I making this assumption?

Interpretations — How am I interpreting this information or this person's response?

Selecting — What data am I selecting based on my biases, views, and past experiences?

Observable Data — How am I interpreting the data observable? The facts.

Imagine walking into a meeting room and seeing someone slam their fist on the table while yelling. You turn to your coworker and ask, "What's happening?" They reply, "Oh, that's just John acting like a two-year-old, having one of his usual childish fits because he didn't get what he wanted." You respond, "No, John is slamming his fist on the table and shouting." The first person's response is clouded with their story about the situation, filled with their beliefs, biases, judgments, interpretations, and perceptions, none of which represent the actual facts.

When an event triggers a reaction, observe how you select specific pieces of information and apply your own meanings and assumptions to it. Notice when you are drawing conclusions influenced by your internal perceptions, opinions, and beliefs. From that point of awareness, you take action. By then, you're far up the ladder, responding based on an emotion or event rather than the data and facts. This becomes particularly difficult during conflicts, where we tend to be high up on the ladder, entrenched in our views and opinions about another person's motives and intentions, many of which may be untrue.

Mindfulness helps you become aware of when you're ascending the ladder. It takes deliberate effort and practice for the mind to refocus on the data instead of getting stuck in reactivity. One wonderful way to apply this concept is to observe your inner dialogue throughout the day. When you realize you're trapped in an interpretation about yourself or someone else that keeps your thoughts high on the ladder, start to shift and climb back down by asking yourself, "What am I reacting to? Am I reacting to my own story, biases, or the actual data?" In that moment of clarity, you become more adept at choosing how to respond. If there is a strong emotional component to your response, use the emotion exercise described in the previous chapter to process the emotion and uncover what you are feeling at a deeper level.

EMOTIONAL INTELLIGENCE

Recognizing and
Managing Your Emotions

Andy's Story - Improving Relationships

My mindfulness meditation practice helps me to be a better leader as Head of Risk and Compliance for a global insurance company in so many ways. In fact, I wonder how I led people before having a mindfulness practice. It enables me to be more grounded and not at the mercy of the potentially overwhelming list of priorities. Previously, my mind would react rather than respond to pressures before I prioritized my mindfulness practice and made it an essential part of my every day. I am much more available and present for those I lead, more able to listen to them, and more capable of empathizing and understanding the challenges they face. It doesn't mean I am perfect or immune, far from it, as I am sure my team would testify! It does, however, mean I can very quickly identify the times when I have acted unskillfully and take appropriate action to apologize and address those situations, as my ego doesn't prevent me from doing that. I am also much more willing to share my vulnerability, as I no longer feel a need to project an image of invincibility. This has helped create an environment where my team is happy to share their vulnerabilities and ask for help, knowing they won't be judged. As a result, we are much closer.

—◗   ◖—

Mindfulness training can reshape our brains to enhance emotional intelligence through focused attention and awareness exercises. According to Wikipedia.org, emotional intelligence is defined as "the ability to perceive, understand, manage, and handle emotions. People with high emotional intelligence can recognize their own emotions and those of others, using emotional information to guide thinking and behavior, and discern between different feelings, labeling them appropriately." A person with high emotional intelligence can adjust their emotions to suit various environments.

The primary components of emotional intelligence, as outlined by Daniel Goleman, an American psychologist, journalist, and a pioneer in teaching emotional intelligence, include self-awareness, self-management, social awareness, and relationship management. These components can be developed and refined through meditation and attention training practices and are essential for leaders. Emotional intelligence can also be nurtured through practice and real-world experiences. Research has shown that the social skills cultivated through meditation practice are consistent with those of individuals with high emotional intelligence. By training the mind to recognize the reality of our experiences and self-correct when we are stuck in erroneous views or self-limiting beliefs, we can better regulate and control our emotions.

When the mind is not overwhelmed by emotions that fuel obsessive thinking, blame, judgment, or fear, we can achieve our goals more effectively. From around the age of 25, most adults engage the prefrontal cortex, the brain region responsible for executive functions, at all times. However, when we experience fear, we temporarily disconnect from the prefrontal cortex. Obsessive thinking is often driven by fear. By releasing fear and other similar thoughts and staying connected to the prefrontal cortex, we become more adaptable and maintain a positive outlook on life. We work better in teams and collaborate more effectively because we can understand others' perspectives without being so rigid in our thinking driven by ego and self-preservation. We develop a greater sense of empathy and become strong influencers. We handle uncertainty and balance high cognitive demands with grace—skills that are highly desirable in leaders.

While this sounds straightforward on paper, how do we actually implement it? When training clients in emotional intelligence, I use the RAIN method as a tool to help leaders process situations in real-time and recognize where they might be attached to a specific outcome, preventing them from seeing clearly. It enables leaders to become aware of their own emotions and transition from a thinking/doing mode to a new mode of observing, feeling, and being. This shift opens the mind to different perspectives, creative strategies, and methods that were previously obscured by emotion, reactivity, obsessive thinking or doubt. It allows the mind to expand and become more inclusive. This method, originally created by Michele McDonald, a meditation teacher in the United States, has been popularized by Tara Brach, a psychologist, author, and meditation teacher. RAIN stands for Recognize, Allow (which I adapt to Allow and Accept), Investigate, and Non-Identification.

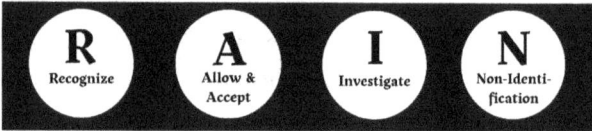

Dealing with a difficult feeling?

Let it RAIN

R	A	I	N
Recognize	Allow & Accept	Investigate	Non-Identification

R

Recognize
What is happening to you right now? Notice emotional reactivity. What emotions are present?

A

Allow and Accept
Invite in and make space for the entire experience - thoughts, feelings, moods, emotions - without resistance. "It is as it is." What most wants your acceptance?

I

Investigate
Explore what is happening in your body and mind. Name sensations. What most wants your attention? What matters most to you about this? What needs are not being met for you?

N

Non-Identification
You are not identified with this experience. This is not who you are.

This method can be used in any situation where someone is emotionally reactive or triggered by a current or past experience. It cultivates self-awareness and emotional regulation, and can be used in the moment or as a regular meditation practice.

Employing RAIN encourages you to lean into the experience as it is happening instead of falling into resistance, avoidance, and aversion. With RAIN, you turn toward challenging thoughts, conflict, confusion, cravings, and sensations instead of avoiding or fleeing from them. For instance, when a strong experience or emotion arises, focus on the somatic response being activated in your body, resisting the urge to intellectualize or obsess over the sensations. Instead, rest in them, connecting with them on a physical level, using simple descriptive language. Let's explore how to use RAIN with the following steps.

Recognize: What is happening to you right now? What emotions are you feeling? You might sense these emotions as physical sensations in the body or as racing thoughts.

Allow and Accept: Allow the situation to be as it is. Accept what is happening right now, even if it feels uncomfortable or unpleasant. Notice any arising resistance. Try a few rounds of breathing, silently saying "allowing" as you inhale and "accepting" as you exhale. At this stage in RAIN, allow all thoughts, feelings, emotions, moods, and mind states to be present without interference or judgment. Observe what arises in your body, mind, and heart, and permit yourself to genuinely feel what you feel. Honor these feelings— they exist for a reason.

Investigate: Observe the physical sensations this experience is causing in your body and name them with one word as they arise, such as tingling, pulsing, pressure, tension, heat or coolness, heaviness or lightness, pit in the stomach, gripping, shaking, contraction, numbness. Welcome these sensations with curiosity and openness. Avoid judging them as "good" or "bad." Simply witness them.

Non-Identification: Don't take it personally. What you are experiencing is just that—an experience. It is not part of your identity. It's something that has happened; it's not who you are. For example, anxiety is just anxiety. Saying, "I am an anxious person," identifies you with the experience and makes it a part of your self-concept. Instead, name it for what it is: anxiety. Anxiety comes and goes. This less reactive approach helps avoid "selfing," where you make something you are experiencing a part of yourself. Let it go. The mind often slips into what's familiar, like slipping on an old, comfy pair of slippers. The good news is you have the choice to break these habitual patterns that no longer serve you. This choice requires dedication and commitment to practice and change the mind.

The good news is you have the *choice* to break these habitual patterns that no longer serve you.

One of my clients, Jimena, was working with RAIN in her practice. A financial executive, Jimena encountered a troubling situation one day at work that left her upset. Her boss called her into the office and asked her to let go of one of her senior employees. While the request itself wasn't unexpected, the short notice of a few days and the news that she would have to take over that employee's duties until a replacement was found, which would require a lengthy executive search, caught her off guard. She asked for some time, and went to her office to practice RAIN. After her practice, she returned to her boss and clearly communicated her needs. She requested additional time before the termination to find a replacement and successfully negotiated a better severance package for her employee.

When Jimena arrived at my office that evening, she was still visibly upset. She said, "I did the RAIN practice and managed to communicate what I needed, but I'm still upset and my stomach is in knots. Why?" I asked her to close her eyes, guiding her through the RAIN steps again. I encouraged her to silently answer the

RAIN questions and feel the physical sensations triggered by the event. After the practice, I asked, "What did you notice?" Teary-eyed, she admitted, "I just want the person I have to fire to like me." After a pause, she added, "I feel so embarrassed that I feel this way." We linked this to her habit of always seeking approval and wanting to please others, identifying the stomach pain as a manifestation of these feelings. This realization was eye-opening for her. Her lifelong reoccurring stomach pain also ceased to exist. This is the power of RAIN. Leading from a need for approval had limited her leadership effectiveness. With this new awareness, she could change her responses by acknowledging and understanding her underlying beliefs.

The more you use it, the easier it becomes to call upon RAIN immediately in moments of conflict or reactivity. For these techniques to be effective, they must become habitual and be used consistently. Otherwise, in the heat of an emotional situation, you may forget to apply them.

RIGHT THOUGHT

Meg's Story - Wholesome
and Unwholesome

Throughout my career as a Director of Community Investments, when I was overwhelmed with workplace issues and exhaustion, quitting my job was a daydream I often contemplated. It sounded like a glorious escape route. But when it came time to leave and start a different life, create fresh routines, and discover a new purpose, fear and paralysis set in. Its claws were deep and held on tightly. The drive and sense of achievement that had permeated my life for 40 years disappeared into thin air. I was adrift.

Over time, my many years of training with Christine came to my rescue, and I grabbed onto what I had learned like a life raft. Having the ability to rest in equanimity, focus on what is wholesome instead of what is unwholesome, and believe in my own wisdom flooded back to me. Stillness found its place in my mind and body, and I allowed it to make a home there. My new life is a quieter, sweeter version of my old one. While I am committed to working on issues I care deeply about, I do it with a new sense of humor and joy and lead from this place. This is a gift to me and everyone around me.

— ◦ —

"Calmness of mind is one of the beautiful jewels of wisdom. It is the result of long and patient effort in self-control. Its presence is an indication of ripened experience, and of a more than ordinary knowledge of the laws and operations of thought."

~ James Allen, *Serenity*

Right thought is a key component of the Noble Eightfold Path in Buddhism, often referred to as right intention. This ancient teaching emphasizes the cultivation of wholesome and beneficial thoughts. Right thought involves nurturing thoughts and intentions rooted in compassion, loving-kindness, and empathy toward all human beings. These positive thoughts promote calmness of mind and self-control. Practicing right thought means letting go of negative and harmful thoughts such as anger, hatred, resentment, and bitterness, which breed discontent. Instead, focus on cultivating thoughts of goodwill, generosity, and understanding towards yourself and others.

In meditation, practicing right thought involves training the mind to see reality clearly, free from conditioned perceptions. It's about developing an unbiased understanding of the present moment or a conversation you're engaged in, without distortions or attachment to outcomes. Right thought is not taught in schools; we learn to cultivate it through meditation and attention-training practices. By practicing right thought, and studying these principles, you gain insight into the true nature of your mind and experiences, leading to a deeper understanding of yourself and the world around you. This practice helps you move away from unskillful, habitual responses towards greater clarity, wisdom, and freedom in your life.

When the mind is caught in "wrong thought," it leads to suffering. Wrong thoughts are mental states that disturb the mind, based on distortions, misunderstandings, or misperceptions. Being trapped in this mindset can result in harmful actions that reinforce negative thinking. For example, if someone believes their worth is solely determined by external achievements or possessions, they may constantly strive for success and material wealth, only to find that it doesn't bring lasting happiness or fulfillment. This can lead to feelings of dissatisfaction, stress, and a sense of never being enough. Distorted thinking limits our understanding, creates conflict, and hinders our ability to cultivate compassion, empathy, and positive relationships. When the mind is filled with wrong thoughts, we might think, "If I push away what I don't like, I will be happy." However, avoidance is never helpful.

Training the mind to return to right thought involves taking action to cultivate wisdom, understanding, and a clear perception of reality. This promotes overall well-being. Right thought includes recognizing the impermanent and interconnected nature of all things and developing a balanced perspective of ourselves and our work as leaders.

Effective leadership requires a mindset of detachment and clear seeing. It involves letting go of ego-driven desires and attachments and approaching situations with clarity, wisdom, and ease rather than personal agendas. A leader's goal is to support the team and the company as a whole. When a leader's mindset is focused on "I, me, or mine," commonly referred to as "selfing," they become stuck with the same thoughts, situations, and circumstances focused solely on benefitting themself. This focus on the self makes thoughts feel more solid, permanent, and fixed. It's essential to realize that things are always changing, so there's no need to make everything about the "self."

Leadership demands flexibility, open-mindedness, and the ability to consider diverse viewpoints. When we cling to wrong thinking driven by our beliefs, and ego, we focus on proving ourselves right, getting what we want, or maintaining control rather than seeking the best solutions for everyone.

This mindset creates significant suffering. When we are stuck in wrong or unwholesome thoughts, it comes from a self-centered perspective with statements like, "I am afraid," "I hate," or "Things will never change," and we may blame others for our outcomes. This way of thinking is exhausting. Attachment to getting what we want and avoiding what we don't want narrows our focus on short-term outcomes or personal gains. This undermines long-term strategic thinking, ethical decision-making, and the ability to build lasting relationships based on trust and mutual respect. Understanding is a crucial skill for leaders. Often, leaders jump into problem-solving mode without taking the time to cultivate understanding before finding solutions.

This ancient story illustrates how we remain trapped in cycles of mental suffering by reliving our experiences:

> Master: "If a person is struck by an arrow, is it painful?"
>
> Student: "It is."
>
> Master: "If the person is struck by a second arrow, is that even more painful?"

Student: "Yes, it is."

Master: "In life, we cannot always control the first arrow. However, the second arrow is our reaction to the first. And with this second arrow comes the possibility of choice."

The first arrow represents our initial experience. The second arrow is the pain we cause ourselves by reliving that experience, whether it's hurt, failure, or embarrassment, leading to additional stress. This second arrow is within our control. We have the choice of how we respond. Life becomes unsatisfactory when we dwell on this second arrow. The only certainty in life is that everything will change. Nothing is permanent. Life's inherent uncertainty means accepting, "It is as it is."

By practicing turning away from wrong thoughts, we become more open to new ideas, feedback, and collaboration, which supports leaders in creating a more inclusive, innovative work environment that fosters acceptance, growth, and success. What we think about, we become. When we think positively, we empower others. Train the mind to reside in right thoughts, and you will change your results.

Right thought involves filling the mind with wholesome qualities and thoughts. Consider the kind of nonsense that often occupies our minds. We often run on automatic pilot, thinking habitual thoughts. Practicing right thought means actively turning the mind around to change our thinking, our relationships, and our daily lives. This brings freedom and allows one to see deeply into the mind.

When we align our minds with right thought, we recognize that it is easier to let go and understand that our perception is not as real as it appears to be. Reflecting on this can help release the grip of struggle, tension, and mental chaos. When we do something that doesn't align with our integrity or create understanding, connection, and goodwill, it is helpful to ask, "Is what I am thinking right thought? Does it lead to the end of my suffering?" By consciously observing your thoughts and their causes, you can mentally shift to a new, positive, and more productive thought, changing your outcome.

When our minds align with right thoughts, peacefulness naturally arises. When aligned with wrong thoughts, restlessness, discomfort, and loathing may arise. If you can trace your thought back to its origin, you have the opportunity to let it go. Ask yourself, "What is its root?" It could be cultural, environmental, or familial conditioning. Creating space around that thought and shifting your attention to something that isn't caught in a story provides a sense of ease. The sense of self is a story we tell ourselves, and it changes all the time. We might have a story of who we are and how we are in the world. Sometimes, we need a story to heal and move through it, but sometimes we hold on to the most awful stories because they feel safe. We may tell the same story of trauma, lack, betrayal, victimhood, or loss for years. It keeps us stuck. It falsely appears safer to hold on to something unhealthy and unproductive than to let it go. This keeps us trapped in old thought patterns and habits that no longer serve us. It can affect our leadership style if our old story leaves us full of thoughts of failure and self-doubt. This type of thinking creates mental exhaustion and burnout.

> *"If we cannot control something, then it is wise to surrender to the experience as it is. When we have pleasant states, we enjoy them but don't cling to them. When we have unpleasant states, we don't push them away. We open fully to the ten thousand joys and sorrows of life, realizing they are all subject to change."*
>
> ~Ronald Charles Denhardt

Wholesome vs. Unwholesome

Training the mind in right thought involves understanding the difference between wholesome and unwholesome thoughts. This practice creates peace of mind. Experiment with aligning your mind to these concepts. During meditation, you can observe two distinct mind states: wholesome thoughts (joy, compassion, understanding, patience, loving-kindness, positivity, ease, peace, acceptance) and unwholesome thoughts (negativity, anxiety, worry, fear, judgment, ill will, resentment, craving).

Silently make a mental note to yourself when your mind is in either wholesome or unwholesome states. Say "wholesome" to yourself when your mind wanders to expansive, positive thoughts. Say "unwholesome" when your mind drifts to negative thoughts rooted in aversion, worry, stress, obsessive thinking, bitterness, or resentment. Then, gently return your focus to the meditation object of your choice, like your breath or body. Alternatively, you can use terms like "beneficial" and "non-beneficial" or "appropriate" and "not appropriate." Choose the words that resonate most with you.

When you notice a thought, ask yourself: Is this thought beneficial? Will this thought create ease or suffering? Is it expansive, positive, creative, or joyful? This practice can help interrupt the train of proliferating thoughts. For instance, if you find yourself thinking about how much you dislike a coworker during meditation, ask if that thought benefits your well-being. Clearly, it does not. If you're ruminating over why you didn't get a promotion, is that beneficial? No. Accepting "It is as it is" allows you to turn your mind toward something more positive.

Additionally, become aware of the physical sensations in your body when you have certain thoughts. Notice the physical sensations produced by each thought. When your mind starts to wander, redirect it to the energetic quality of the thought in your body. Every thought creates a response in the body. Joy might produce lightness, tingling, space, and ease, while anger may cause contraction, burning, rapid heartbeat, and restlessness. Pay attention to all these sensations, even when the mind is free from thought. Observe, what does your body feel like when there is no thought? Be discerning about what thoughts you choose to entertain because your thinking is affecting your physical body. For example, if you are frequently dizzy or nauseous, what are the predominate thoughts in your mind? Begin to understand the connection between the way you think and how you feel physically.

Ask yourself, "What is my mind doing right now?" several times during your meditation to recalibrate. Observe if your mind is dull, active, sleepy, foggy, clear, or angry. Be curious about what is present or absent in your mind. It's a misconception that we are meant to be stopping thoughts when we practice training our mind and meditating. Thoughts will always be there—it's the nature of the mind.

When I am stuck in a particularly sticky unwholesome thought, I recall a teaching by Joseph Goldstein, one of the first insight meditation teachers in the United States. He asks, "What is a thought?" When we examine it closely, a thought is little more than a wisp of nothing. However, thoughts can dominate our lives. Making thoughts the object of meditation helps us understand the nature of our minds, awareness, and the power of delusion. When I'm stuck in an unwholesome thought, it usually involves delusion, attachment, or ego, and I make a mental note of it. After taking note, we must return to our breath or body, our centering object of meditation.

In practice, it's helpful to investigate mindfulness of thought. This involves noticing when you are in the thought process. We often become aware of a thought after it ends. Sometimes we notice it at the beginning, sometimes in the middle. Train your mind to wake up the moment a thought begins, and observe what is present in each moment. When you do this, you are practicing correctly. Notice everything without judging, competing, or attaching.

Notice and reflect on what happens after a thought arises. Does it disappear, fade, stop, or do you become stuck in it? Notice the tone of your mental note. Are you kind to yourself, or is your inner tone harsh? This reveals your mind's attitude, which reflects in your leadership. Meditation practice always teaches you something about yourself. This self-discovery is one of the greatest gifts of practice.

Consider this story:

> A Sufi figure from the mid-13th century, Mullah Nasruddin, was both a fool and a wise man. One day, he was in his garden, sprinkling breadcrumbs around the flower beds. A neighbor asked, "Mullah, why are you doing that?"
>
> Nasruddin replied, "Oh, I do it to keep the tigers away."
>
> The neighbor said, "But there aren't any tigers within thousands of miles of here."
>
> Nasruddin responded, "Effective, isn't it?"

Our meditation practice is like this. We train the mind to keep the "tigers" (darkness, negative thoughts) away. It's a cultivation of right thought toward being emotionally regulated and intelligent, keeping unproductive, unskillful thoughts away. The tigers represent unwholesome thoughts.

Practice: Drop It

Use the phrase "Drop it" when your mind falls into the habitual pattern of trying to intellectually figure everything out or control the outcome. There's a profound freedom in realizing that you don't have to solve everything during meditation. Accept that it's not everyone else's fault you're experiencing something challenging. Simply be with your thoughts, sensations, and emotions. This is your mental break. Be curious about the tone and nature of your mind. When we are lost in thought, it gains power over our lives because we are unconscious, reacting from habit, reactivity, and past painful experiences. Mindfulness and habit cannot coexist. When mindful of our thoughts, we realize we have a choice in which thoughts to follow and which are merely habitual.

There is a continuous ebb and flow in practice, and eventually, it becomes embedded in your life. Everything turns into practice. Sylvia Boorstein captures this beautifully in a dharma class at Spirit Rock Meditation Center in California: "I think of my whole life as one long practice of attention and awareness. This doesn't mean I always know if I'm breathing in or out at each moment or am aware of how everything in my body feels. My practice, moment to moment, is to be attentive to the arising of negativity: unwholesome thoughts, greed, hatred, and delusion. If I notice it, it goes away. This creates space in the mind that allows for something sweet to come."

DON'T KNOW MIND

We Don't Have to Know Everything!

Erin's Story - Don't Know Mind

I work in a high-stress, volatile industry, which led me to turn to a meditation practice. Having tools like the "don't know mind" practice has helped me find quiet despite the uncertainties I face every day. The practice of meditation has also offered me better clarity, as I have given myself the time to sit with ideas and listen to my intuition rather than react immediately out of emotion. My leadership style has evolved to better understand why someone may be reactive. By listening carefully and distilling down what need isn't being met, I can better communicate and provide for my team.

My practice has transformed this feeling of drowning into a feeling of gratitude. I see a full life with incredible children and an amazing career opportunity. I practice to understand where the greatest imbalances reside so I can take action to correct them, while accepting that some level of imbalance is just reality. My meditation practice offers me understanding and joy—a better perspective.

"Worries are pointless. If there's a solution, there's no need to worry. If no solution exists, there's no need to worry."

~ Matthieu Ricard

There is a wonderful teaching in the Buddhist tradition inspired by the concept of "freedom from views." It's known as "don't know mind." In the Zen tradition, it's called "the practice of not-knowing." This practice involves maintaining an open-minded state and non-attachment to fixed ideas, views, or beliefs. It's about letting go of preconceived notions and resisting the urge to know everything or seek certainty. It encourages openness to others' opinions, perspectives, and beliefs. The "don't know mind" concept invites us to step back from what we think we know about ourselves and the world, centering ourselves in the present moment.

Imagine what it would be like not to worry about what's next, what's going to happen tomorrow, if the stock market will crash, if your portfolio will underperform, how the meeting will go, or if you will win the big account. It's much lighter and more freeing to rest in a don't know mind. There's less energy needed. It can be scary because we believe we must hold tightly to our beliefs and control what's next, and this thinking can be exhausting, leading to burnout. The mind loves control and order; this is its nature. It doesn't like uncertainty, so it clings to what is certain. However, life is inherently uncertain. "It is what it is."

Heidi Grant and Tal Goldhamer wrote in their *Harvard Business Review* article that our brains are not built for uncertainty. "Given that habits and recognizable patterns are kind of its 'thing,' the brain evolved to be uncertainty-averse. When things become less predictable—and therefore less controllable—(like a pandemic, economic crisis, organizational restructuring) we experience a strong state of threat." The brain craves recognizable patterns and feels threatened by uncertainty, even when no actual threat exists. Understanding this natural response and using our practice tools helps us navigate through uncertainty.

Everything is impermanent and changes from moment to moment. Nothing is fixed. By embracing life's uncertainty and practicing the "don't know mind," we can alleviate the suffering that comes from trying to control and grasp certainty. Recognizing that we don't have to know all the answers lets us approach life with curiosity instead of contraction and fear. How do we counteract this tendency to seek certainty? We practice the concept of the "don't know mind" and train the mind accordingly.

For some people, travel often triggers worry and anxiety, making it an excellent opportunity to practice "not knowing" and use our practice to calm emotional dysregulation and proliferating thoughts of fear, doubt, and worry.

Ralph, a Senior VP in the Benefits Administration, traveled frequently for work. He shared, "I had severe anxiety-related symptoms around the entire travel experience, from setting my alarm to wake early, finding airport parking, arriving on time, and what would happen when I landed. My mind would be in a ruminating cycle of worrying thoughts: 'What if I can't find parking? What if I miss my connecting flight?' I tried anxiety medication, but it made me feel out of it. I decided I didn't want to take medication anymore or feel this way. I thought, 'It's kind of ridiculous that I feel this way!'"

After attending a corporate training I led at his place of work, where he learned about meditation and its benefits, Ralph started practicing with body scans and sitting meditation, where he learned to label his thoughts. The guided practices gave him confidence. He recounted, "There was one time I had to travel for work and had to be 'on' for my clients immediately after landing. I didn't have time to relax in my hotel room or have a drink by the pool to decompress and numb my anxious feelings. I put on headphones and listened to your 15-minute guided meditation practice. After listening twice, I felt better. Now, I practice on my own for 5-10 minutes almost daily and incorporate walking meditation at the airport to further settle my mind."

Practice: Don't Know Mind

During meditation, notice when the mind starts planning, doubting, or questioning, and say "don't know" silently to yourself. The mind often believes it knows how another person feels, gets stuck in fixed views, questions how we will get everything done, worries about a medical condition, not getting a raise, or fears being laid off. When thoughts of uncertainty arise, softly note "don't know" and return to your breath or meditation object. Practice this method daily in addition to your formal practice. It's a continual process. When wondering what will happen in an upcoming meeting or if your child will get into college, say "don't know." This trains the mind to let go of ruminating and worrying when it starts to spiral. Practicing the "don't know mind" requires patience and a willingness to let go of control and certainty. Cultivating this practice brings greater flexibility to the mind, allowing more wisdom and compassion to arise.

Life becomes stressful when we want things to remain the same. What changes from moment to moment cannot provide lasting happiness or security. Aligning with this truth teaches us that safety comes from within. When we rest in not knowing and accept uncertainty and impermanence, the body and mind relax. The heart opens. It becomes easier to be kind, generous, and courageous because we no longer need to protect ourselves or build ourselves up to be something other than our true self.

IMPROVING COMMUNICATION

Makes Us Better Leaders and Fosters Better Relationships

Lori's Story

Some of my favorite tools that have been most helpful and beneficial to me in my work as a project manager in the healthcare industry are not only the mindfulness practices but also dedicating the necessary time to build this muscle consistently. One of the most helpful tools was writing and reciting "Just like me." I would recite it consecutively three times before my meeting with my boss. Doing this gave me a calmness I hadn't experienced before. It allowed me to see my boss as a fellow person, 'like me,' which resulted in empathy and clarity.

Another key tool Christine taught me was to name the negative feeling or emotion that I experienced when receiving feedback. Each time that negative feeling or emotion arose, I would name it to myself. By doing so, I could compartmentalize it, preventing it from 'tripping me up' during my meetings. This, in addition to reciting 'Just like me' before my meetings helped me and eventually changed the dynamic of my relationship with my boss.

This has helped me become a better project manager and leader. The mindfulness practice provides scheduled time to refocus, offering a calming period to regain perspective. It has given me the focus and ability to concentrate on what I need to do and be less distracted. It has helped reduce my tendency to be impulsive, especially during decision-making. It has increased my emotional intelligence, as I explained above—it allowed me to step back and consider others' perspectives and to help me quiet the negativity and self-doubt in my own mind. Most importantly, as a leader and project manager, it has given me greater resilience by helping me accept and adapt not only to change but also to feedback. I can hear the feedback; I can accept others' perspectives, but I do not have to accept it as truth. My knee-jerk reaction to resist or offer justification has been minimized, and I no longer allow it to overwhelm me. I have truly reached a place of peace with myself.

"Eighty percent of the people who fail at work do so for one reason, they do not relate well to others."

~ Robert Bolton

Relationships are the foundation for success as a leader, and effective communication is key. People do not want to follow a leader who doesn't listen or communicate clearly and honestly from the heart. Communication is a give-and-take process. Good listening forms meaningful connections with others. If you can't listen, you can't truly understand the other person. Leaders need to be aware of their own internal processes and let go of self-centeredness and ego to respond skillfully. This self-awareness comes from dedicating time to meditation practice. Listening inwardly to your thoughts, beliefs, and patterns affects how you engage in communication and lead. Leaders must stay connected to their internal presence at all times—whether caught in an emotional outburst with a colleague or trapped in self-doubt and unsure how to respond to a critical situation. In either scenario, being internally connected with full awareness and a stable, centered mind allows you to respond wisely instead of from habit, emotions, or biases.

Improving communication with others at work, home, and in life is possible through mindful listening. Mindfulness cultivates attention and awareness while strengthening our ability to listen to others. Often, we listen to our inner voice rather than the person speaking. Mindful listening involves paying attention with a receptive attitude to what the speaker is saying and tuning into their body language and emotions. With consistent meditation practice, we learn to listen well and stay connected to our internal presence. This practice helps train your mind to listen to the voice in your head without being derailed by it.

Reflecting back what is being heard increases understanding and improves interactions with everyone in our lives. We create positive relationships by mindfully listening and not reacting to what is being communicated. This fosters deeper understanding. Practices like "Just like me," that cultivate empathy, are essential and will be explored further in this chapter. Empathy is a critical skill that allows one to listen well and understand another's viewpoint. If you are caught in a negative story about a team member not pulling their weight, it's harder to find empathy for them. Empathy removes barriers by dissolving the sense of self-orientation versus others when communicating and listening.

Humanize the other person by empathizing with their experience, perspective, and alternative viewpoints. This practice promotes understanding. Every person is unique and brings their individuality to every situation. Empathizing does not mean condoning, agreeing with, or approving harmful actions. We can only control our internal responses to what is difficult, whether it be a challenging boss, work environment, conversation, etc. Humanizing another person prevents you from falling into an "I'm right, you're wrong" mentality. It builds connections by respecting their position, understanding their motives, and fostering inclusivity instead of isolation and feelings of separateness.

> *"When someone really hears you without passing judgment on you, without trying to take responsibility for you, without trying to mold you, it feels good. When I have been listened to and when I have been heard, I am able to re-perceive my world in a new way and to go on."*
>
> ~ Carl Rogers, Psychologist

The definition of "listening," according to Ridge Associates, one of the largest leadership training organizations in the United States, is "a set of skills that demonstrates you understand and can interpret what is being communicated from the speaker's frame of reference." It's a skill set, which is encouraging because it means you can learn and improve these skills.

How do you know if you are a good listener? I receive a wide range of answers to this question, but rarely do I hear the correct response. We only know if we're good listeners if somebody tells us we are.

The frame of reference means putting yourself in another's shoes. When someone communicates with you, they speak from their perspective, not yours. It's about understanding how the other person sees something, not how you see it. You might have a very different perspective, and your mind might automatically react with thoughts like, "I can't believe this person thinks this way!" or "I need to give this person advice."

> Anisha shared how her practice changed the way she interacts with her children, colleagues, family, and friends. Understanding others' frames of reference and why someone may act or feel a certain way gives her the opportunity to respond differently when a need isn't being met for either herself or the other person. She can adjust her communication to be better understood. Sitting with reflective questions before reacting has empowered her to respond with effective solutions.

One of the ways we can track conversations mindfully is by practicing attending skills. Attending skills, as defined by Robert Bolton, author of *People Skills*, are all nonverbal and they involve the following:

- Posture of involvement such as leaning forward
- Head nods
- Eye contact
- Facial expressions
- Gestures

How do you know if someone else feels heard? Eye contact is a major indicator that you are paying attention when someone is speaking. If you are looking over someone's shoulder while they are speaking, or checking your Apple watch every time it buzzes, the person is not going to feel heard. However, combining all nonverbal gestures will help the person feel fully heard. Establishing a meditation practice naturally enhances your listening skills by training your mind to quiet the inner voice and not distractions. When you learn to let that voice or distraction wait, you become more present during conversations. You are less likely to think about your response and more likely to truly hear what is being said.

Maintaining attentive silence while following and tracking a conversation is crucial. A consistent meditation practice hones the ability to stay silent even in situations where we feel the urge to speak up quickly. Doing so could derail the person talking.

If you notice that someone is hesitant to talk, you can invite them to share their story using "door openers," as Robert Bolton describes. These invitations encourage continued speaking. Examples include: "I'm interested," "I'd like to hear more, please continue," "You look upset, would you care to talk about it?" or "I have time to listen if you want to talk." As the person shares, provide brief prompts to show you are listening. Prompts like "hmm," "yes," "tell me more," or "Oh, I see" indicate engagement. The key is not to interrupt with your thoughts or advice but to let them express themselves without judgment or making it about you.

It might feel like active listening when you engage with the speaker, but giving advice, asking questions, or offering reassurance can indicate that you aren't truly listening and can be off-putting. These communication modes are frequently overused in today's culture. Sometimes we operate on autopilot, offering advice that helped someone else in the past, but it might not apply to this different person. Interrupting someone while they speak is also problematic. Why not wait? What's the hurry? Meditation practice teaches us that there is time. Take it all in. You might mean well by saying, "Don't worry, everything will work out fine," but this can come across as flippant, as if you don't recognize the significant impact the situation has on them. Are you really listening to what they need to convey, or are you putting them into a predefined box? Consider responding in a way that shows they have been truly heard. To show that you are listening, try using their own words in your response. If you want to give advice, offer empathy first and then ask, "Are you open to advice?" This gives them a choice, making them feel heard instead of receiving unwanted advice.

Reflecting

After listening to someone's story or conversation, it's essential to reflect back on what you heard to ensure you are on the same page and understand them. According to Ridge Associates, "reflecting" is defined as "the listener briefly states in his or her own words what's the core of what is being communicated." To do this, we search for the core meaning—the essence of what the speaker truly wants you to know.

Reflecting isn't just about repeating the same words in a conversation. That just shows you have a good memory. It's about capturing the feelings and context being communicated. How can your response match the emotion the other person (or group) is expressing? When possible, make your response brief and use language that indicates you have understood the emotional content. By considering the other person's feelings, you demonstrate empathy. You can show this by matching the tone of the other person. If someone is quiet, respond quietly. If they are very excited, try to match that energy.

Years ago, when I was teaching mindful listening at Tufts University, I asked the group to reflect on a story I shared about my son, which was meaningful and personal. I intentionally told the story in a scenic way, with tangents, to make it challenging to track the core message. I asked for a reflection back from the group.

A participant volunteered. He stood up and reflected back to me the core of what I was communicating, capturing the essence and root emotions of my story. As he reflected back, my eyes teared up, my heart opened wide, and I felt heat fill my body. When someone truly listens and understands you, you *feel* it. There is a somatic response in the body when you feel heard, understood, and witnessed. It takes training to do this because our minds are often scattered and reactive with hundreds of thoughts running in the background, making it difficult to find the core of what someone is communicating.

A key aspect of mindful listening that is often overlooked is that listening does not mean agreeing or approving what is being communicated. The goal of communication is to cultivate understanding—not to make someone agree with you, see your perspective, or take your side. It's okay not to agree.

It's important to never fake understanding or tell the speaker you know how they feel. You can never truly know how another person feels. What's important is recognizing how your speech lands inwardly (inside yourself) and outwardly (how it is received). When you are not paying attention, you may say things you regret. The goal of a leader is to have self-control and make others feel heard, valued, and appreciated. Imagine a coworker says something that upsets you. Instead of responding emotionally, you have the ability to respond with curiosity and refrain from responding unskillfully when you have these tools onboard.

Practice: Reflecting Back

How does one reflect? An example of a reflective statement might be, "It sounds like you're struggling to manage this client's demands, and they're blaming you for being behind schedule, which is upsetting you." Or, "You feel angry because you didn't get the raise you believe you deserved." Another example could be, "From your perspective, you feel unappreciated and unrecognized for completing that project ahead of schedule and within budget, and that makes you mad."

Hijacking a conversation, however, is not reflecting. Have you ever experienced telling a story, only for the listener to take over by saying, "The same thing happened to me!" and then proceed with their own story? When someone responds with, "I know what you mean," and continues with their own experience, this is hijacking. This is often done subtly, and the hijacker might not even realize they are doing it. Once, while teaching a session on reflection, someone shared a story of something that had also happened to me that day. I jumped into autopilot mode, replying, "Oh my goodness, that happened to me," and began to tell my story. I stopped mid-sentence when I realized I was hijacking their story! It was a valuable teaching moment. Our minds are conditioned to habitual communication modes and can easily revert to old habits like interrupting, even as we strive to develop new ones.

If a conversation becomes too overwhelming for your nervous system to handle or you can't follow the discussion, it's important to interrupt politely rather than pretend to understand or abruptly end the conversation without explanation.

What if you don't have time to listen? This question comes up often. It's crucial to communicate if you don't have time to listen at that moment. Show respect and kindness. If someone catches you between meetings and shares a difficult problem, but you lack the time to listen attentively, it's okay to say, "I really want to listen to you. Can we revisit this tomorrow when I have more time?"

Mindful presence is essential in any dialogue. It allows leaders to access wisdom and empathy during difficult conversations or when their nervous system is reacting out of habit. If your natural tendency is to avoid challenging conversations or reviews, practice the techniques suggested in this book. Avoidance, shutting down, or exploding are habitual responses that need addressing to foster change. Establish a consistent meditation practice to cultivate curiosity, patience, stillness, and kindness in your responses, training your mind to react differently.

Leadership involves more than being a visionary, giving directives, and solving problems. It includes being somewhat aware of the experiences of other people and letting them know they have been heard. As you intentionally improve your communication, you will notice changes in how people interact with you and what they share about their needs.

Practice: Just Like Me

A powerful way to cultivate empathy and compassion, and to strengthen your connection with others, is through a practice called "Just like me." This technique, a form of non-violent communication, can be an effective tool for conflict resolution. When someone's behavior is different from what you want to see, or they speak in a way that is not mindful, or they are not performing to their best ability, it's natural to harbor negative thoughts about them. "Just like me" helps reframe these thoughts, reminding us that we are all sharing a universal experience of life. As mentioned in the introduction, we all suffer at times. Recognizing that someone might be going through personal struggles can affect how they are behaving and make a huge difference.

Here are some "Just like me" phrases to help you start this practice. Think of someone you are about to converse with whom you perceive as difficult. Visualize this person and reflect on the phrases below, repeating them to yourself. You can personalize the practice by inserting the person's name in place of "this person."

- Just like me, this person wants to be happy and healthy.
- Just like me, this person desires to feel understood, accepted, and to belong.
- Just like me, this person has dreams and ambitions they wish to achieve.
- Just like me, this person has experienced pain, sadness, and loss.
- Just like me, this person has faced challenges in life.
- Just like me, this person seeks moments of peace and tranquility.
- Just like me, this person aspires to do well and be loved.
- Just like me, this person wants to be free from suffering.

Focusing on these phrases as a self-awareness practice helps overcome the usual obstacles that create feelings of separation, isolation, or difference from others. It changes the way we communicate. We begin to see similarities with others, noticing what unites us rather than what divides us. When I taught this at a large conference, an attendee asked, "What if this person doesn't want to be happy?" Another remarked, "This person likes being angry." Consider what it might be like to be this person. Do you really believe they prefer anger over happiness? Such thinking stems from ignorance and confusion, creating a sense of separation. We all have bad days and can be caught in our internal suffering longer than we would like, leading to anger and affecting our communication. This doesn't mean we want to remain that way.

This practice requires training. To make it a default mode of thinking, start with neutral people. Sometimes it's easier to practice with people you don't know personally while sitting in traffic, in a coffee shop, on a train, or in a store. For example, as each person in line orders coffee, reflect on the phrases for each individual. Notice how this shapes your mood and day.

A human resources director at a large university told me this was the most valuable practice she learned. She taped the phrases to the back of her phone and repeated them for each person who entered her office. Handling diverse requests, intense conversations, and legally challenging situations daily required her to see each person as unique and separate from the previous individual. She could be firing an employee one minute and hiring another the next. Using "Just like me" phrases helped her humanize each person and approach each interaction with a fresh perspective.

I have successfully used this practice to resolve conflicts within teams where communication had broken down and avoidance, judgment, and blame were prevalent. "Just like me" is also effective in family systems where communication has become argumentative and hostile. It is most effective when practiced in the presence of the other person or team, leading to greater understanding when the experience is shared afterward. Daily practice enhances this understanding further.

CONCLUSION

"Once I accept myself as I am, then I can change."

~ Carl Rogers

By focusing on the principles outlined in this book, leaders can learn to lead from within, empowering themselves to take action, achieve their goals, and make meaningful contributions to others. Effective leadership arises from embodying qualities such as self-awareness, confidence, kindness, empathy, understanding, and a positive attitude. We can transform our lives by changing the way we think. As humans, we possess tremendous mental power and the freedom to choose our thoughts. When we focus on positive thoughts, we feel good. Conversely, when we focus on negative thoughts, we don't feel as good. It's that simple. Everything has both "good" and "bad" in it. Nothing is inherently good or bad; it is our thinking that determines its nature.

> *"Man is a psychological being, a thinker. It is not what he feeds upon physically, but what he feeds upon mentally that he becomes. We become the embodiment of that which we mentally feed upon."*
>
> ~Neville Goddard

The way we think generates feelings in our bodies, influences our actions (whether physical or verbal), and ultimately produces results. Everything begins with a thought. What you think and believe shapes your reality. You can change your outcomes by changing the way you think. You have the power to choose thoughts that motivate, inspire, and uplift you—and others. Shift your internal dialogue and replace low-energy words like struggle, overwhelm, and exhaustion with more empowering terms like expansion, growth, challenge, and ease. Unlock the immense potential of your mind to empower, lead, and thrive by training it effectively.

I invite you to embark on a journey of training your mind, getting to know yourself more deeply, and understanding how your mind operates. Your results in work and life reflect your mindset and habitual nature. Leadership is challenging, which is why not everyone pursues it. You have to believe in your potential to lead. With consistent training, what once seemed difficult will become easier, altering your perception.

Once you decide to engage in a transformative cognitive practice like mindfulness meditation and attention training, you will discover all the time, resources, and coaches you need. Whatever you require, you will attract. You have the potential to achieve anything, but you must decide, commit, and start where you are with what you have. No excuses. And without feeling bad about your starting point. Recognize that you are beginning something new, which takes courage. Meditation is not something you do only when you feel like it or when you're having a bad day. It is a lifelong daily practice. Repetition and persistence are key. The only time to change your thinking and your life is now, in this present moment.

As you read in the client stories throughout this book, mindful training for leaders has been invaluable. When corporations invest in mindfulness training, they cultivate happier, healthier, and more effective leaders who are high-performing, inclusive, and empathetic. A team is only as emotionally intelligent as its leader. Invest in your leaders' mental training to create the results you desire.

Sarah's Story

I am a working mom. No matter what I do, everyone wants more—my children, my team, my family, my friends, my charitable causes, my children's school, and so on. There isn't enough time in the day (and I include night in that calculation) to do everything. I am the mom who enlists my sister to bake cookies for the bake sale. When it comes to signing up to volunteer at school, I have to select, "bring in gift cards for the teachers" (and, honestly, my sister delivers them for me too!). The mom is the household CEO even if the dad is the primary parent. You should see my morning on the day of summer camp registration. Calendar blocked, I play varsity level when the camp slots open on the website, even if I am on the train or mid-air. I FaceTime into the kindergarten school plays at 9 a.m. even if I am traveling for work and happen to be in multiple time zones away. At work, my competition is often males with no children or males with stay-at-home moms. How can I possibly compete? It is overwhelming.

Trying to make everyone happy, trying not to forget anything. Trying to be perfectly composed with confidence and gravitas even if I am thinking to myself, "It is raining outside. Did I leave the windows open?"

As I walk into my house at 8:05 p.m. on a Tuesday, it looks like we were robbed. The robbers had a party and left the kitchen a mess. The milk is likely open on the counter. That is likely the moment when the groceries were delivered two minutes before I had to leave, and, in my haste, I spilled blueberries all over the floor. At times, I just have to leave them to make my train. Let's not even talk about my laundry situation. I support my family, so work is paramount compared to household chores.

My practice has transformed this feeling of drowning into a feeling of gratitude. I see a full life with incredible children and an amazing career opportunity. I practice to understand where the greatest imbalances reside so I can take action to correct them while accepting that some level of imbalance is just reality. My meditation practice offers me understanding and joy—a better perspective—even when the blueberries end up in the compost.

You only have one precious life. What do you want to make of it? What do you want to create? How do you want to inspire others, your children, and everyone you meet daily? If you want to be healthy, focus on healthy, wholesome thoughts. If you want to increase your energy, think uplifting thoughts that expand your perspective. You are the deciding factor.

If you want more joy and less chaos, stress, and burnout in your life, master your mind and practice all the techniques outlined in this book. Train your mind, practice loving-kindness daily, process your emotions instead of suppressing them, and silence your inner critic. Focus on increasing your emotional intelligence by using meditation tools like RAIN to navigate difficult situations and events. Study the section on Right Thought and constantly observe your mind to catch unwholesome thinking as soon as it begins. Redirect your mind to rest in wholesomeness. Improve your communication by practicing mindful listening and building meaningful connections with others. Let go of what you cannot control. No one knows what will happen tomorrow. Life is this way...it is as it is.

ACKNOWLEDGEMENTS

Thank you to all my teachers who have guided me throughout the years. I am deeply thankful to Insight Meditation Center in Barre, MA for providing me the space to sit, be still, and absorb the wisdom of the teachings over many years which inspired me to write this book.

A special thanks to my friend and mentor, Tara Healey, for over 20 years of support. Your guidance in my practice and introductions to the teachers I needed to learn from have been invaluable. I appreciate your encouragement to attend longer retreats and for the constructive feedback you provided on various chapters, often at short notice. You have always been a wise sounding board during pivotal moments in my life and practice.

I am also grateful to my dear friend, Elaine Stokes, for always being by my side every step of the way through this journey, and in life, with all its ups and downs. Thank you for offering me the space in Vermont to write and for helping with brainstorming and providing valuable feedback on the book. You are a true leader, my friend.

I feel blessed to have an amazing community of friends, colleagues, and family who have supported me throughout this process; you know who you are. Thank you, Jim, for your patience in editing, proofreading, and providing suggestions through countless revisions of this book.

This book would not have been possible without the many clients, students, and corporations who attended my workshops, classes, and trainings, whose feedback inspired me to write and to lead from my practice. I hope this book offers meaningful insights into your mind.

WORKS CITED

Bertin, Mark. "Living with, and Loving, Your Imperfect Life." *Mindful*, Mindful.org, 22 July 2016, https://www.mindful. org/living-loving-imperfect-life/.

Bolton, Robert. *People Skills*. Touchstone, 1986.

Brach, Tara. "Feeling Overwhelmed? Try the RAIN Meditation." *Mindful*, Mindful.org, 17 Feb. 2023, https://www.mindful. org/tara-brach-rain-mindfulness-practice/.

Goldstein, Joseph. *Mindfulness: A Practical Guide to Awakening*. Sounds True, 2016.

Goleman, Daniel. *Emotional Intelligence: Why It Can Matter More Than IQ*. Bantam Books, 1995.

Grant, Heidi, and Tal Goldhamer. "Our Brains Were Not Built for This Much Uncertainty." *Harvard Business Review*, Sept. 2021, https://hbr.org/2021/09/our-brains-were-not-built-for-this-much-uncertainty.

Hall, John. "Why Attention Management Is the Secret Sauce to Success during the Pandemic (and After)." *Forbes*, 19 Apr. 2020, https://www.forbes.com/sites/johnhall/2020/04/19/why-attention-management-is-the-secret-sauce-to-success-during-the-pandemic-and-after/.

"Heavy Multitaskers Have Reduced Memory." *Stanford.edu,* https://news.stanford.edu/stories/2018/10/decade-data-reveals-heavy-multitaskers-reduced-memory-psychologist-says. Accessed 1 July 2024.

Goddard, Neville. *Out of This World: Thinking Fourth-Dimensionally.* Martino Fine Books, 2010.

"People Skills Training Course." *Ridge Training,* 23 May 2019, https://ridgetraining.com/training-services.

Rumi. *Selected Poems.* Translated by Coleman Barks, Penguin Classics, 2004.

Sofer, Oren Jay. *Say What You Mean.* Jiu Jing, 2020.

Spirit Rock, https://www.spiritrock.org/.

Van Der Kolk, Bessel. *The Body Keeps the Score: Brain, Mind, and Body in the Healing of Trauma.* Penguin Books, 2015. https://www.besselvanderkolk.com/resources/the-body-keeps-the-score.

Weiss, Leah. *How We Work: Live Your Purpose, Reclaim Your Sanity, and Embrace the Daily Grind.* Harper Paperbacks, 2019.

ABOUT THE AUTHOR

Christine O'Shaughnessy is the founder of Mindful Presence, which provides executive coaching and mindfulness training to corporations, groups, and individuals, helping them thrive in emotional intelligence, leadership, and creativity. By integrating mindfulness into executive coaching and leadership training, individuals can cultivate core social competencies that drive growth and enhance the way they speak, listen, and act, leading to more mindful communication. Christine is passionate about helping clients develop better responses to life's challenges rather than reacting automatically and habitually.

Her areas of focus include enhancing emotional intelligence, thinking strategically and motivating others, achieving goals in a guided, efficient, focused, and profitable manner, responding appropriately to high-stress situations, effectively managing difficult employees, interpersonal differences, and other conflicts, developing self-awareness, self-regulation, and emotional self-control, increasing empathy, understanding, and the ability to manage relationships, boosting creativity and the ability to innovate beyond self-imposed limits, and improving overall quality of life and well-being.

Christine's understanding of the effects of stress on health as people advance in their careers has inspired her to incorporate mindfulness into daily life as a vital tool for managing stress, increasing self-awareness, and regulating emotions, as well as addressing issues like addiction, anxiety, depression, pain, and long-term illnesses. She works with a wide range of executives and corporations, including non-profits, investment and financial management firms, technology companies, healthcare organizations, and educational institutions. Her focus is on helping individuals achieve work-life balance while enhancing performance, communication, and fostering greater behavioral flexibility.

Christine brings a wealth of knowledge from her previous career as a corporate executive into her mindfulness training, guiding individuals to become more mindful leaders in the workplace. She has served as the Managing Director of a search and consulting firm, the Director of Sales for a software company, and as a Vice President and Senior Credit Analyst at Loomis, Sayles & Co., an investment management firm in Boston. She holds a BA in Finance and an MBA from Babson College. Christine has completed intensive training programs including Proctor and Gallagher's six-month leadership development program, Thinking Into Results, with Diamond Mind Consulting and is RYT200 certified. She has been teaching workshops and leading corporate retreats since 2004. Additionally, Christine is also a Senior Mindfulness Instructor for Point32Health, the parent company of Harvard Pilgrim Health Care and Tufts Health Plan, and the co-creator of Harvard Pilgrim's online instructional yoga videos.

Additional Resources

Mindful Presence in Leadership: Releasing Burnout, Chaos and Stress is not written to be a one-time read. It is a resource for you to refer back to over and over again.

Repetition is the key to all learning and is necessary to change the inner landscape of your mind.

This book is meant to be shared and recommended to others who need it.

Keep it on your desk at work, on your nightstand, in your kitchen. Return to it and the exercises within frequently. The tools offered in this book will only work if you take action. I have guided meditations under the LEARN tab on my website: www.mindfulpresence.net.

You are welcome to download to meditations and visit my website to learn more about my training and coaching.

I am here to support you.

NOTES